Seven Breaths

Seven Breaths

Stepping into Your Power of Choice

Amos Lovell

Felton, California

Seven Breaths: Stepping into Your Power of Choice
Copyright © 2012 by Amos Lovell

All rights reserved. No part of this book may be reproduced, stored in a retrieval system, or transmitted, in any form or by any means, electronic, mechanical, photocopying, recording, or otherwise, without the written prior permission of the author, except in the case of brief quotations embodied in critical articles and reviews.

The material in this book is intended to educate. The author does not advocate changing or stopping any medication or treatment protocol prescribed by your health care professional. Please consult your medical practitioner or therapist before undertaking any new exercise or healing regimen. No expressed or implied guarantee as to the effects of the practices contained herein can be given, or liability accepted.

Cover and interior photographs by Craig Lovell
www.eaglevisions.net

ISBN 978-1-935914-10-5

Printed in the United States of America

Additional copies available from:

www.riversanctuarypublishing.com

RIVER SANCTUARY PUBLISHING
P.O Box 1561
Felton, CA 95018
www.riversanctuarypublishing.com
Dedicated to the awakening of the New Earth

ACKOWLEDGEMENTS

People ask me what inspired this book and truly there were a few specific hours that sparked the project; however, this work is the result of a lifetime of learning and experience and so my deepest gratitude is to life itself. So, also, do my thanks go out to so many people who have been a part of my life, love, and learning.

Thank you, Elizabeth, for being my dear and actively loyal friend. Thank you, Robert, for your solid committed support. Thank you, Charlie, for your passionate heart centered leadership and modeling. Thank you, Lee, for insisting on being big, and of course for Star Trek night. Thank you, Jack, for thinking more outside the box than I do. Thank you ,Toni, for the incomparable magic. Thank you, uncle Fred, for showing me it's cool to be a great car mechanic. Thanks to my men's group for insisting on having my best interest at heart. Thank you, Kirsten, for making babies with me and for agreeing with me about the basics. Thank you, James, for living "I love you." Thank you, Todd, for being passionately connected to me and loyal. Thank you, Austin, for being my son and for the strength of your love and your natural leadership. Thank you, Jenny, for being my daughter, for your passionate heart, and your innate ease in the world.

Thank you life, for the ride. It's been truly amazing.

CONTENTS

Ackowledgements 5

Introduction 1

Chapter 1: How to Use This Book 7

Chapter 2: Breathing 11

Chapter 3: The Power to Change is in You Now 19

Chapter 4: Stepping Actively Into Change 29

Chapter 5: From a Certain Point of View 41

Chapter 6: Shifting a Habit 53

Chapter 7: Inviting You to Thrive 63

Chapter 8: Making It Real 69

Chapter 9: If You Get Stuck 73

Breathing Exercises 81

    A. Conscious Breathing 83

    B. Affirming Your True Nature 85

    C. Inquiry – Noticing What is Really True for Me 92

    D. Moving Through 101

    E. Release 104

    F. Welcoming Goals and Changes – Activities 109

    G. Welcoming New Perspective – State of Being 117

    H. Gratitude and Forgiveness 128

INTRODUCTION

Australia 2007

Several years ago I was traveling in eastern Australia in springtime with my son Austin. We had landed in Sydney, bought a car and were set up for camping. After a few days we found a beautiful isolated spot to camp near a waterfall about 20 miles from the coast.

It was a peaceful time, a time to slow down, notice our surroundings, and relax. It was cattle country – mostly flat with a few rises and clumps of trees here and there. Kangaroos hopped through the camp several times a day, cows mooed, and the bird song was new and amazing. A person could open up and expand there, so we did.

We spent the days walking around, talking sometimes and taking in the beautiful newness of the Australian countryside. Each evening around sunset hundreds of birds would begin a symphony of sound with varied songs, staccato highs and trills, whoops and calls, and all with cows mooing a low base line in the background. It truly filled my ears with pleasing sound and my heart with appreciation for the performance Mother Nature created and allowed me to witness.

As beautiful as it was it also was new and unusual. Having grown up in northern California, I also grew up with the nature sounds of northern California as a backdrop to my life. These sounds had been an integral part of the flavor of my days all my life. I was not aware how much I relied on those sounds to validate my sense of "normal" or feeling OK. I was awakened several times during the night to new animal calls. I realized that at an unconscious level those background noises ongoingly informed me of what animals were around, what they were doing and if I was in danger. It was a bit unsettling getting used to new ones.

My son and I had a peaceful, relaxing time together. Good talks and good quiet time. After a few days we decided to move on. So after packing up our camping gear we each set off separately on a farewell walk preparatory to leaving.

I set out into the field with my eye open for bones. (I collect bones.) After a mile or so I saw a little rise with a dozen trees and two big rocks; one flat and one standing about 15 ft in the air. I decided to stand on the flat rock in front of the upright one and do some deep breathing. I held out my hands and took a deep breath. As I did I thought to myself simply "I am here." That breath relaxed me – slowed me down a bit. I took another deep breath and thought, "I am connected to everything around me." My senses expanded. I began to feel the elements around me – the air, the trees, the sun, the rock I was standing on. My awakeness was growing.

I breathed deeply a third time, sighed and thought "I am here now." I began to feel palpably connected. Energy flooded into my feet and hands, almost like I was becoming a part of my surroundings.

On the fourth breath birds arrived to roost on the branches a few feet from my head. My state of mind began to shift. My spine tingled. I thought "I can feel the deep connection with everything: the elements, animals, people, seasons, hot and cold – the flux of my planet (and the universe)." I was part of the flow.

On the fifth breath, all the birds started making noise at me, and I thought, "I am at cause. What I choose to believe is amazingly powerful" and then I made noise to join the birds. I engaged purposefully in the flow.

On the sixth breath I knew myself as a creator, that my beliefs and intentions generated the world I perceived, and I made a big noise, and the birds made a big noise with me. I was losing my sense of separation.

On the seventh breath I inhaled deeply and was filled from the ground up with huge energy that I could feel through my body and up my spine and into my head filling all my senses with an ecstatic tingling. I knew that I was so connected and that I was at cause and completely at effect of life simultaneously. My body felt like it was floating. I shouted as loud as I could. The birds were silent, and I heard a triple echo of my voice.

Amazingly there was nothing around to echo at me! No mountains or hills for many miles!

After the 7th breath I stopped to listen and feel what had happened.

My body was vibrant and tingling. I could see/feel that I had been given something powerful coming from the earth, from my surroundings. Something profound had been offered to me. Seven breaths had begun.

My body was high and energized and my thinking was clear. My awareness was greatly expanded, and as I walked, it seemed more like I was floating back to camp.

Austin and I started driving to the next town. The intense feeling in my body subsided, but there was an impression left, an impression of importance and of moment. Not only had 7 breaths been a gift, but it was a gift to share; something to offer people. It was a simple, profound way to tune into life, connection, belief and creation. It was a way to access power, presence and ability as a human being.

Serendipity – Here you are now

Why are you here reading this right now? It is likely because something in this book will benefit you in some way.

I believe we tend to show up in situations, meet certain people, go through joys and sorrows, witness life's dramas or feel and notice things that will teach us or benefit us in some way. As we have these experiences we can pay attention or not. We can take them into our minds, hearts and bodies to be fully experienced....or not.

The choice is always yours to make. If you choose to pay attention, to breathe the moments in, life becomes richer, more flavorful, more interesting. It can be joyous and fulfilling, or it can feel difficult and uncomfortable. Both serve to help us grow, to teach us, or simply to allow us the opportunity to experience another amazing moment. A moment of self, or a moment of connection with that which is other than self.

Life is immense. The opportunity to connect with life is also immense. People, plants, politics, rain, rocks, rivers, sun, smiles, smells, food, fears, fantasies, animals, memories, visions, joy and despair...the list goes on and on. Connecting with any of these things or feelings or experiences is an opportunity for ecstasy. There is spiritual presence in all, and there is ecstasy in joining with that spiritual presence.

So...will you choose to breathe life in...to invite that ecstasy? If you do, when will you start? Now?

It is not difficult. It is actually quite easy. You can carry on with your whole life, and still breathe in the ecstasy and fullness of more and more moments as they come by. Life becomes more vibrant and colorful, more real and more fun!

In the end there is actually no reason not to start now. The thinking mind can create reasons, like – I don't have time, or I don't deserve it, or even – this will threaten my survival. But it won't. You have the time and the capacity to breathe, and to feel and have that moment of pure connection. Right here right now. You can decide and you can change. Take a breath! Think...*I am here!* You have started. It's that simple.

In most any situation there is a way to benefit. Something to learn, to notice, something to enjoy, something to release or to receive. It is simply about deciding to be here, notice what is here in this moment inside of you and outside of you.

No matter what has happened or how you feel, you still get to start now. Right here and right now you get to start living in full open connection to the immense gift of life. Breathe!! I extend my hand to you in invitation. Will you take it? Let's journey together!!

Chapter 1

HOW TO USE THIS BOOK

As a pathway to empowerment: choosing what you want

If you know what you want, or what you want to move toward in life, turn to the "Welcoming" section and choose an exercise. Relax and invite yourself to easily recognize a good match for you now. Pay attention to your heart and body as well as your mind. Trust yourself. You will know when you have found a good match. There may be more than one. Try the exercise three times a day for four days. See what happens.

As a pathway to self knowledge: Finding out what you want or who you are

This book contains many exercises designed to assist you in finding out what you want or what is really true for you. Look in the "Inquiry" section and try one that seems right.

As a resource for guidance: Spiritual signs, information or direction

This book can be used as a "random" tool for finding an answer or a new idea right now, like picking a card from a Tarot deck. Flip through or browse through the book and see where your fingers or eyes stop. Read there. When I do this, I often find a message that is appropriate to my current need or situation. Trust that your inalienable connection to life will lead you in a useful direction. This method uses the book like a reading from a tarot deck or like noticing signs or messages from your environment.

Alternatively, as you read through the philosophy part of this book, pick an idea that provokes interest or resistance or an emotional reaction. Do the exercise associated with it, and see if you end up in a new or useful place. Trust yourself. You may experience feelings or thoughts that are uncomfortable at first. Remember, this can also lead you to a higher and better place.

As a grounding exercise
To invite calm, full presence now and groundedness, look in the "Conscious Breathing" or "Gratitude and Forgiveness" sections of the exercises for a good match and take a few minutes to focus on youself

As a ritual or opening/closing for a group gathering
Choose a statement of being or of intention for your group to focus attention to a common theme, or use a series of breaths to create a connected, relaxed way of being together.

To shift emotions
Help yourself or someone else calm down, get present, invite enthusiasm, release stress, open the heart, relax the body, release anger, release fear.

Guidelines for your breathing practice

Start by getting comfortable in unrestricted clothing if possible. Choose the exercise you want to practice with, and remember:

- You can speak your intention aloud or think it silently.

- Each intention and breath can be repeated until it sits well inside you.

- Don't wait for your mind. If your body or heart feels complete, move forward.

- To intensify your practice, look into your eyes in a mirror, breathing and speaking your intention aloud.

- One intention phrase is often enough. Simple is good. Simple is easy. Simple works!

- Stop in the middle of an exercise if you feel done – you are at choice always.

- Feel free to *move* your body around, or *touch* anywhere on your body, or make *sounds*. Add body movement or sound to any exercise as it occurs to you.

- Take purposeful breaths. Yawning is also a great way of breathing with intention. It clears the body without involving the mind. This is very desirable.

- If you forget or space out, this usually means you are right on target. You are focused on exactly what you need. Gently return to the exercise.

- Rewrite or reorganize any exercise to fit you perfectly. Choose phrases from two or more exercises and combine them to suit you best.

- Pick one intention phrase the really works well; combine it with a body movement or sound and do it randomly during the day. (I put my fingertips over my heart and say *I am here now* or *I am loved and accepted* several times a day.)

- Write your own intention phrase. If you need help creating an intention that is simple and positive, look in the "Welcoming" section in Chapter 5 (p. 48) for examples. Remember to keep it simple.

- You may contact me to get an exercise designed for you personally at (831) 915-5182 or *amoslovell@yahoo.com*

Chapter 2

BREATHING

Breathing and specifically breathing on purpose has huge potential as a vehicle for health, presence and change. After the beating of your heart, breathing is the activity we do the most in life. Usually we don't pay much attention to breathing. It stays unconscious. It is, however, the simplest conscious activity we can do. It is also the simplest way to purposefully activate change, stimulate the physical body, and move quickly into clear present thinking. Conscious breathing is a powerful tool.

Breathing on purpose or conscious breathing

What does it mean to breathe on purpose? Simple. Try this right now. Take in a breath. As you blow out simply feel the air as it passes over your lips. That's it! That simple activity: noticing the breath as you exhale is purposeful or conscious breathing (see Basic Breathing 1 at the end of this chapter). You can use this simple focus to move toward health, clarity, or any change. Remember: Life works. It can be as simple and powerful as you allow it to be. Combining your breath with your intention can take you anywhere you want to go.

Breathing for alertness, presence, and clarity

To function well, we all need a good supply of oxygen to the brain. Breathing just a little deeper than usual is the quickest way to get oxygen to the brain now.

The better the consistent supply of oxygen, the better the brain works. Oxygen to the brain is affected by blood sugar level, rest, stress, hormones, clear blood vessels, physical health and simply breathing enough. Try this right now: Pause, notice your breathing and simply breathe 10% more than you usually do for about 30 seconds. Just a little deeper than normal. You are putting more oxygen into your bloodstream. What do you notice about thinking and alertness? Try it for 2 minutes. Now what do you notice? Try Basic Breathing 2 (at the end of this chapter) to bring alertness for 5-10 minutes or…

> **Exercise: Breathing deeper (A2 p. 83)**

So if you are tired or stressed or upset or want to think clearly now or stay awake, try breathing a bit deeper for a few minutes. If you want to clear out an emotion like fear or worry or overwhelm, or if you need focus and good thinking, try Basic Breathing 2.

As I have gotten older, it has become more difficult to stay alert while driving late at night. I used to play the radio loud or engage someone in conversation to stay alert. On a road trip recently I started breathing deeper, just a little. I found it kept me awake quite easily. Drinking more water helps too.

Breathing for health

Supplying an adequate or abundant amount of oxygen to your body stimulates the organs, augments healing, optimizes the metabolism, generates physical energy, clears stress, allows you to process food better, helps you sleep, helps you think clearly, stimulates creativity, and helps you be present in your body in this moment.

Purposely breathing deeply for 5 minutes once or twice a day will generate noticeable changes in these areas within a week. Sometimes within a few days. Of course twice a day is going to be more effective than once a day. Try Basic Breathing 2 or 3.

Breathing for change

Breathing is tied to all our emotions and behavior. When you have certain feelings, you will tend to breathe a certain way and if you change your breathing in the middle of a thought or feeling you can change your reaction. For instance if you are afraid, you tend to stop breathing fully. Picture yourself on the edge of your seat watching a scary scene in a movie. Your belly can become tense and breathing shallow. If you breathe deeply, your body tends to relax and the tension and fear will dissipate. If someone has said something upsetting to you and you want to respond, we all have heard the advice to take a deep breath or breathe three times, because the breathing helps the instant reaction dissipate so we don't say something potentially harmful to ourselves or another person.

As you breathe purposely and add intention you begin actually rewriting or reforming the biochemical and vibrational signature of your body and mind. Your history and your beliefs are stored in your body and mind like a recording, so as you breathe with purpose or with a specific intention, you can actually alter this recording. As you do, your thinking, beliefs and reactions will change. What happens for you in your life will change too.

As you alter the recording, thoughts and feelings may rise to consciousness for review or release. Congratulations! Try not to avoid them. They may be uncomfortable or painful or scary, but in the end if you welcome these feelings, they may seem more intense briefly, and then will pass. Accepting them will help you move on, to change. Welcoming a difficult feeling, even if it is scary, is acknowledging or affirming your authentic self.

Deanna came to me saying she was experiencing periodic pains in her belly sometimes including feelings of fear for no apparent reason. She assured me she was not sick. Asking a few more questions she revealed that when her belly hurt she sometimes thought of her boss at work but assured me that they were friends.

During an accelerated breathing session, she remembered an incident in High school when she had been cornered in the girl's bathroom and threatened physically by 4 other girls. She had been so frightened at the time and that emotion was so overwhelming that she had blocked out the memory completely.

The pain in her body was signaling her. Deep consistent breathing had brought the memory up for review and release.

As the memory arose she stopped breathing deeply and opened her eyes, looking at me feeling panicked. I assured her that here now she was safe and that here now she had me as an ally. With this input her breathing slowed. She calmed down, but was still not willing to revisit the memory of that incident.

I led her into purposeful breathing for about 5 minutes simply repeating "I am safe." As she began to feel safe, it also became safe to revisit the painful feelings of fear for her survival from that old experience. She allowed those feelings of fear to be present and the resultant pain in her body to be present. It was quite uncomfortable for her. Allowing the difficult feelings to be there and repeatedly checking to assure herself that she was safe now, she was able to move through the pain and panic.

Breathing deeply while affirming safety released the tension she carried in her body. She began to recreate physical ease in her belly and brought herself back to choice (power) about staying present in her body and feeling safe at the same time.

Further talk about her female boss at work revealed Deanna's thoughts that even though they were friends she sometimes got the sense that there was competition between them for who was the more valuable employee, and that in a worst case scenario Deanna could get fired.

Fear for her own financial survival had triggered the belly pain connected to the memory of her being physically threatened (physical survival) in High School.

> **Exercise: Welcoming a feeling (F15 p. 114)**

Breathing for vision

Deep breathing can bring you to an altered state of consciousness. It can make you feel high, or allow you to access a different reality or new perspective. This altered state can inform you about yourself and about life in a new way and can be transformative and healing.

The breathing exercises can also unlock your truth; bring it up out of your body for review. Sometimes old patterns of thinking or feeling will simply present themselves for re-evaluation or re-decision as you breathe. Sometimes the body will tingle or cramp as it releases tension or holding. Sometimes the mind/spirit will give you a vision that portrays a metaphor or provides a pathway that your unconscious mind can follow to health or ease or balance. Aspects of your life that you took for granted or perhaps had not noticed recently can become important to look at.

Basic Breathing Exercises

1) Wherever you are, whatever you are doing, simply start breathing about 10% more or deeper than you usually do. If you lose track and stop, simply start doing it again.

   Try breathing 10% deeper for 1 minute 5-10 times during the day for a week.

> **Exercise: Breathing deeper, A2, p. 81)**

2) Get comfortable so your belly and chest are free to move. Make sure that you are situated so that you cannot fall or hurt yourself if you get light headed. Take deep full breaths at the rate

of 3 seconds in and 3 seconds out. Breathe consistently for 3-5 minutes. Use a timer if you can. When you over-oxygenate you tend to lose track of time. As you breathe, feel free to move your body around. Touch or hold yourself if you are drawn to do so. Freely make any sounds that come up. If you get too light headed, slow down so you stay conscious. You may notice places of tension or tingling in different areas of your body. These may be touched or held or massaged to move stuck energy through, or for no reason at all.

3) Do the above exercise at the rate of 2 seconds in and 2 seconds out, or even faster. Take full deep breaths stretching the muscles in your chest and belly just a little as you fully inhale and as you fully exhale. You may become light headed. Slow down or stop to stay conscious.

Guidance for the breathing exercises

- Remember that breathing 10% deeper is usually not noticeable by others. You can breathe a little deeper and invite clarity of thought or clearing of emotion in most any situation.

- Deep breathing can cause tingling, tightening of muscles, spontaneous emotion, physical discomfort, physical and emotional ecstasy, and relaxation, just to name a few responses.

- Since thinking and creativity are often enhanced while you breathe deeply, you may want to have a paper and pen handy so you can write down any ideas that come up. With your ideas written down you can keep them and then relax back into *not thinking* to finish your breathing exercise.

- Feel free to move any part of your body or touch any place that you are drawn to and also to make sounds as they come up. The body becomes the recording device for the experience of daily life. Emotion or trauma can be held by the body awaiting release. Breathing can release it. Accelerated breathing can also clear the mind and can relieve pain or illness. Touch and sound also facilitate this clearing.

- Deep breathing or over-oxygenating can alter your state of consciousness. This shift of perspective can be experienced as the natural result of quieting the thinking mind, opening the heart, as a window into another lifetime or another dimension, or even as a message from spirit. However it makes sense to you, I invite you to allow this new perspective to open the door for you to ease, health, growth, self knowledge and change.

- Deep breathing in some instances can give you visions or other experiences that seem foreign to your regular point of view. This is life offering you new perspective to facilitate growth and healing. Try to welcome this newness. Remember that you don't need to understand. Letting the mind figure something out is only one way of inviting change. Perhaps allowing the unconscious mind to move without guidance or allowing spirit to move you is enough. Understanding can arrive later. It is not necessary as a starting place. Life works. Trust!

Chapter 3

THE POWER TO CHANGE IS IN YOU NOW

Choice is power

You are at cause and you are in the moment of choice always: right now, this second, about every aspect of your life. Choosing is your present moment connection to your power. Your power to choose what you think, believe, feel, and do and therefore what your life will look like or feel like.

Being at cause simply means that if you are dissatisfied with a part of your life you have the power to cause change starting now. You can change belief about what is true. You can change your belief about how or if you need to show up.

You are a creator and therefore create all aspects of your life always. You have the choice to fail or succeed in your own terms, or to *change the terms* so your view of failure or success changes.

You are at cause and at choice about it all.

At cause does not mean *to blame*

Being at cause for all aspects of your life does not mean that you are to blame if things are not working out well. Knowing that you are at cause is actually liberating. This knowledge empowers you to create something new, to realize that you have the power to shift at any moment.

Mary spent many years unhappy in her marriage. She and her husband never seemed to enjoy each other for long. Although they seemed to agree on what was important in life, they would have a few laughs, and then long uncomfortable silence most of the time. They argued occasionally, but not enough to feel threatened. He became more and more focused on work, and she was consumed by thoughts of guilt. She wondered what she was doing wrong that caused the distance between them. Did she need to be friendlier? Become a better lover? Have a baby? Work harder at something? She could not figure out what to do, and the pressure of guilt inside her got bigger and bigger.

One day she exploded emotionally. She yelled and called him names and blamed him for a failed marriage. She told him she wanted a divorce. Briefly she felt better. She had shifted the burden of blame from herself to her husband and without the little voice in her head telling her it was her fault, she could think more clearly. Talking to a friend she realized that she had been very unhappy for a long time. Her dreams about how to connect with each other and the community, where to live and what a family looked like were very different from her husband. He was a good man and also was not that interested in her dream.

Talking later with her husband she realized that though they loved each other, they were not meeting each others needs. Staying together was continuing to create stress for them both. Each felt that they were moving further from ease and happiness by ignoring parts of their own true nature in order to please the other.

The emotional explosion allowed her time free from the little voice in her head telling her it was her fault. She made a decision to move away from her husband based on her real needs.

Without being burdened by the weight of blame from the little voice in her head, she finally had time to think clearly about what she really wanted. As she identified these wants and needs more clearly, the little voice telling her she was at fault disappeared. Without the blaming of herself or her husband, she was able to once again identify what she had admired about him when they met, still knowing that they were actually not a good match.

Blame takes a lot of mental and emotional energy without serving anyone well. Some people have been taught and believe that blaming themselves or others is an effective way to stimulate change. It can be. Blame can generate a feeling of obligation to the blamer (even if it's yourself) so the feeling of obligation has enough influence to get someone to make a change. Still in the end the change is made because the person blamed is at cause in her own life and has decided to make a change. Blaming does not alter the ability to choose, it simply creates drama and demands emotional energy around the choice.

The blamer is saying "I want you to choose thinking or behavior that matches my terms and I am willing to coerce or even threaten you into that choice" You can always say no. The choice is still always yours.

I have never seen evidence that there is any kind of cosmic judge that gets to decide what is right or wrong or how well you are doing, or that can give or withhold blessings or favors based on your performance. There is, however a little voice in your head that does judge and decide these things. That voice will influence the direction of your life whether it really serves you well or not. It will reward you or punish you based on it's beliefs about right, wrong, truth and worthiness.

What is *true* or *real* can change, and when it does, the experience of your life can change with it.

Consider others whom you know whose beliefs are different than yours. They tend to experience the *truth* of how life works that they expect to experience. Consider aspects of your life and values in which the *truth* has changed over time. I will guess that your experiences changed right along with your view of the truth.

It is OK to tell the little voice to be quiet or to take a break or to come back when it has something positive or truly useful to say. It is

OK to inform that little voice that it has been operating on outdated or even false information and to teach it new and useful information. You are actually in charge...even of that little voice.

> **Exercise: Quieting the little voice (G10 p.120)**

Choosing a story instead of a change

Sometimes instead of choosing change we choose a story about why we can't change. My life is too complicated to embrace this change. My spouse will freak out if I do this. I will get fired. I don't have enough time. I don't have enough money. This is too hard. People will dislike me. People will resist this decision. I am not OK like I am – wrong body shape, skin color, education, experience.

One day, Tasha, the woman I lived with said to me. "You know you slouch a bit when you walk." I responded by talking about my flat feet and that my feet pointed outward when I walked and the exercises I needed to do to change all that. The story I had chosen was that I had to perform certain tasks in order to change. She listened for a minute and then said "Why don't you just walk straighter?" In that moment I realized that it was really that simple. I decided to do just that. Over the next two months just by deciding to walk straighter my slouch disappeared and I gained ½ inch in height.

I had been attached to the story about what I needed to do to change instead of simply moving into the change.

So if you have a change that you want, one that you are clear about, and there seems to be resistance to the change, or obstacles seem to appear to block your way, look at yourself. Ask yourself "Do I really believe I can have this change? Is it really OK? Am I holding on to a story that says I cannot change in this way?"

> **Exercise: Finding all of my story (C23 p. 99)**

Be aware that even if your conscious mind says OK, sometimes your unconscious mind does not. Sometimes your resistance to change will be obvious and understandable. Sometimes it will make no sense at all. Either way, you can move through it. In the end, with intention your unconscious mind will move in the direction your conscious mind leads. You can write a new story.

> **Exercise: Moving through resistance (D3 p.102)**
> **Exercise: Moving through stuckness (D4 p.102)**

Survival and fear

If for any good reason or for no reason at all, you know or sense that your survival is at stake, then, for most of us, the rules about what to do change. We will do what ever we must to insure our survival. Being confronted with a situation that challenges survival, physically or emotionally, often includes fear as a new motivator and seems to reduce our options. We feel separated from full choice. Fear, especially about survival, distorts thinking and may separate us from our highest ideals or full ability.

For instance: Even though I love you and have kind and gentle thoughts about you, I may strike at you verbally or physically if I think you are going to leave me because it feels like emotional death.

Even though I am a successful and fully functional part of the work world, I may freeze inside when thinking about being fired because it feels like I will not be able to survive physically.

Be careful to identify when it feels like your survival is at stake, knowing that this can shift your access to full choice.

> **Exercise: Bane of fear (D1 p. 101)**

Creating change

Creating change is made up of three basic elements: identifying what you want to change, allowing yourself to choose and accept the change and then acting positively to create new beliefs and engage in new behavior.

What do you want?

How's your life going? How does that picture look to you? Do you like it? Is it the one you want, or do you want something else? Do you even know what you want? If you are reading this now I will guess that you are interested in changing some aspect of that picture. Great! If you know what that is, great! If not, when will you choose to identify what you want to change? And then when will you invite that change? If not now then when?

Take some time for yourself simply think well about what you want. If you are not used to considering yourself this way, then perhaps it is time to start a new habit. Try taking time to do this each day for a week, even if only for a few minutes. Write it down. Explore your wants and needs by yourself or with a safe friend.

Remember that as you step into identifying what you want, sometimes the point is to identify specific things that you want. Sometimes instead, the genuine need is not a specific item, but a lifestyle or perspective that generates specific things. For instance, I could say "I want a million dollars." For me, however, my real want is to not worry about finances. A million dollars would be liberating in one way. I could use that money to pay for the life style I want. It would also bring with it the need for time and attention to manage and keep that amount of money working for me. This might be worrisome in itself. I then ask myself. How many other ways are there to live and not be worried about finances? Perhaps there are ways to do this that I haven't even thought of. Paying good attention to my own values and gifts, I would be better off to simply set intention for financial ease, and let the universe respond with the specifics. I would likely be happier with the result.

> **Exercise: Finding what I want (C20 p. 98)**

This is also a place to be careful. As you identify what it is you want, do your best to come from an authentic place. It is easy to slip into wanting things that we have been taught to want by family, teachers, the media or our culture. Some of these may align with your true desires and some may be actually foreign to your nature and therefore disruptive or too demanding to be beneficial. This means that some changes or activities can demand so much more effort or energy than the benefit they provide that they leave you depleted.

Some activities or goals demand tremendous energy and attention. If the journey or the end product aligns with your true nature it can be wonderfully feeding and satisfying. If it doesn't, the effort can be draining or even make you sick.

> **Exercise: Identifying the change I truly want (C9 p.95)**

Choose things that will feed you, align with your true nature, fulfill your genuine desires, fulfill your life purpose and use your natural gifts. If you choose wants and desires from an authentic place, you will usually find that you meet your practical needs at the same time. You really can have it all. Life can work for you. You can believe it. It is true.

Jim, a chiropractor I knew, was about 45 and had been in practice for 2 years. I asked him how he had come to his profession this late in life. He told me that he had been working for the post office for many years and realized that he was unfulfilled and becoming numb inside from his job. He had always fantasized about being a chiropractor. One day he thought to himself "Four years from now I could have finished chiropractic school or I could still be working in the post office. There will be challenges from going to school, but I will likely be happier and more fulfilled if I do." So he made the decision and went to school. I asked if he was happier and he grinned and said "Oh yes I am." I asked if it had been difficult getting through school. He said "At times, yes, there were new challenges for my family and myself and sometimes they were difficult, and I kept in mind that becoming a chiropractor was my heart's desire. When I remembered this, I found that I soon found the help I needed or the solution to a problem."

He identified a want from an authentic place and allowed himself to make a change.

Identifying a desire or goal and then committing to that change sends a message to the universe. It says "I allow myself and my life to bring about this change." When you are clear about what you want, look out, life will usually rush to give it to you.

Choosing something that matches your true nature…your values, perspectives and gifts makes the change even easier. If you choose a goal that aligns with the true you, you will likely find that you easily identify pathways to your goal and learn what you need to know to accomplish your goal.

Exercise: Indentifying my authentic desires (C22 p.99)

Allowing change to happen

After you decide what change you are inviting, make sure you will really allow yourself to move forword. Ask yourself: Do I have permission from myself or the little voice in my head to have this change? Do I need help with permission? Will my heart and body also allow this change?

> **Exercise: Checking for permission (C14 p.96)**
> **Exercise: Giving myself permission (G16 p.122)**
> **Exercise: Allowing what I want (G7 p.119)**

Sometimes *now* is simply not the right time. Sometimes it just *feels* like now is not the right time. Check out what is true for you.

> **Exercise: True, not true or maybe true? (C12 p.96)**

Remember sometimes as we ask about permission the answer is "No" and even though there is no reason it should be "no," we cannot allow ourselves to change. Sometimes, fears, agreements or beliefs are hidden from our awareness. Still, acknowledging the "no" is the first step to opening the door to "yes".

> **Exercise: Checking for unknown blocks (C24 p.100)**
> **Exercise: Releasing all blockage to change (E5 p.105)**

Chapter 4

STEPPING ACTIVELY INTO CHANGE

Now that you have decided what you want and you can allow yourself to move forward, it is time to identify: what steps to take that work well for you and that lead you to new perspective and what activities are the best ingredients to your change.

> **Exercise: What works best (C21 p. 99)**
> **Exercise: Stepping into change now (F21 p. 116)**
> **Exercise: Inviting change (F19 p. 115)**

Be kind and gentle with yourself as you look for next steps to change your life. Old habits can stick around and show up for redecision over and over. They are *habits* after all. There is no cosmic judge hanging around to condemn you if you need reminding or if you reengage in old habits. There is only the little voice in your head.

Think well and gently about yourself. Set goals that you can reach, and commit to steps that you can do. As you think and plan, find signposts that identify your change and write them down. Also include celebration and acknowledgement for yourself. Any change that you welcome and want deserves celebration. Just the decision to move foreword deserves celebration.

Resistance to change

If as you go, you take note of the places you are habitually stuck or disallow yourself to engage in new habits and perspective, then these difficulties or "bumps in the road" become points of learning or places to clear. As you welcome these difficulties, bring your attention to them, and move through them, you shift and as you shift you feel lighter, more centered, your thinking becomes clearer and more authentic. The result is an opportunity to engage with perspective and behavior that comes from your true radiant self. Life looks and feels better. You change naturally.

Sometimes we avoid difficulties or feelings or fear or anxiety around difficulties. Interestingly if you welcome or literally breathe in a difficulty or fear, it will usually intensify briefly and then subside. You may experience intense feelings. Having those feelings or thoughts will allow the fears to dissipate. In other words welcoming the feelings around difficulties will allow them to pass more quickly.

> **Exercise: Welcoming emotion (G11 p. 120)**
> **Exercise: Identifying a fear (C2 p. 92)**

You are in charge

You are in charge. You always have been. You are a creator. You create what your life looks like and feels like and manifests (or womanifests) like in each moment. You have the ability to positively or negatively affect all of your life all of the time by what you decide to think, feel and do.

Life works. It is designed to work and always works. You get what you believe you will get.

Your body is meant to be healthy so it is designed to heal and can always heal, even terminal illness and long term changes of your body chemistry. You can change your relationship to health.

Your situations and relationships are completely up to you to design. You can have whatever connections you want: loving, gentle, stressful, difficult, competitive, supportive, etc.

You get to decide what is valuable or what is satisfying for yourself even if others do not agree. You get to decide when to struggle and when to have ease. You decide what is success and what is failure. Reevaluating this can change your life!

Your emotions will pass and change. Some of us believe that when we have a feeling, especially a strong one, that this feeling, because it moves us emotionally, is the best basis for decision and action. Though emotion is an indicator that some aspect of your life is demanding attention, perhaps emotion is more of an informer, telling you to reconsider rather than the basis for immediate action or reaction. If someone is rude to you or even abusive, this may make you angry or scarred. Does your anger or fear make sense of being rude or abusive in return? Though you may feel that a similar response is appropriate or justified, or will make you feel better, usually this simply perpetuates a cycle of behavior that serves no one well. Breathe!! Then ask instead: What are my best thoughts and desires for my self and for this person? Perhaps these are a better basis for decision and action.

Exercise: Pick from the following questions those that fit you and write down the answers:

- How will you proceed differently today? What beliefs or behaviors do you choose to release?

- What beliefs or behaviors do you choose to keep and what newness will you invite?

- What can you do or think or be, right now, to begin creating the life you want? Remember that simply thinking differently is the beginning of change and can be a huge step forward.

> **Exercise: Welcoming (F14 p. 113)**

Keep your self safe

Remember that you are at choice always. If someone is repeatedly harsh or abusive, you have the choice to negotiate better treatment or to leave or to disconnect from them. Safeguard your self, your internal balance and sense of peace in your own terms.

> **Exercise: Keeping safe (G13 p.121)**
> **Exercise: Keeping safe while feeling emotion (G12 p.120)**

You can start having what you want any time you allow yourself to. Some of your beliefs may no longer serve you and might get in the way of what you want. Indeed you may find that they are actually no longer true. For example, many people believe that long term primary relationships will become a burden, or dull or unfulfilling; become a fact of life to be put up with. If you believe this or are in a primary relationship that looks or feels like this, ask yourself, Does this belief about relationship still serve me as it is? What parts of this belief or this relationship would I change now so that it will serve my needs better? You can shift your beliefs about what is important any time you want to. It's OK to change your mind.

Your beliefs and perspectives generate your ability to perceive success and to engage in success.

You attract whatever you think about and feel about in every moment. (This is the message of the film *The Secret*)

Conscious and subconscious

Your subconscious mind is part of you. As part of you it has a role. The role is to confirm your beliefs, to help you get what you want, to support you and to please you. Functioning at its best in that role the subconscious always says yes. It says yes to everything. Its says yes to what your conscious mind says and is says yes to every other thought you have, purposeful or not, including your misgivings your fears and your worries.

For instance if your conscious mind says "I want to be prosperous; I want to create financial security," your subconscious mind says "Yes, of course, and what else?"

So then whether you think to direct it there or not, perhaps you also think, "Getting financially secure is difficult." Your subconscious mind says "Yes, you can have that, what else can I do for you?" Then you think, "Not only that, but the economy is in trouble and that makes it even more difficult." So the subconscious mind says "Great! You can have that too, what else?"

Perhaps your mind thinks, "In order to do this well I need support, I need someone to show up for me in a certain way, or I need to accomplish certain tasks in my life first. Perhaps I need money or to get things better with a relationship or have a better resume or a new outfit, or go on a diet etc., etc." (the list goes on). Of course your subconscious mind says "Yes, of course you need to do these things first, and what else?"

Perhaps you are terrified that if you don't succeed financially you won't survive, so you stay frozen with fear. Your subconscious mind says "Yes you can have your frozenness and your fear. What else?"

Perhaps you also worry that its going to be tough to get what you want and your subconscious mind, wanting to please you says "I see that this worry is important to you. Yes, you can have that too."

Part of worry is that worry takes up a lot of your time attention and energy and your subconscious mind goes right along with it because as you spend this time and energy the subconscious mind gets the message that it is important to you. It always says, "Yes, what else can I agree with you about?"

In this situation there are many things that your subconscious mind is agreeing to than your conscious mind would not agree to if asked.

For instance, do you really need to lose 10 lbs or repeatedly think about how hard this will be, or worry several hours of each day in order to move in the direction of financial success? Probably not. Yet this is what you spend your time thinking and what you offer your subconscious mind as most important to focus on, so that is what you get back. Your subconscious mind says yes and supports you in achieving worry and confirming your fears and putting conditions in front of you as tasks to accomplish before you can have what you want.

You can spend more time focused on difficulties and fears than on what you want.

Your subconscious will always support your choice about what is most important by noticing what you choose most often to think about and react to. Then that is what you get more of.

The more thoughts and feelings you have that align with your conscious goals, the more accessible those goals will be.

The learning mind responds best to simple direction: Reminders, activities and affirmations about what you consciously wish to be true. For instance, if you want financial success, try thinking *Making more than enough money is easy*, or *My life will come through with the ideas and support that I need*. Look at Chapter 8 – Making it Real.

Another way to lead your subconscious mind in the direction of alignment with conscious goals is to link your goal with your personal values. For instance *I love my family and I know that financial stability will give them ease*.

So, picturing your spouse or children relaxed and happy will lead your subconscious mind to success.

> **Exercise: What doesn't align? (C25 p.100)**
> **Exercise: Contradicting old beliefs (F22 p.116)**
> **Exercise: Aligning the conscious and subconscious (G31 p.127)**
> **Exercise: Linking success with my values (G32 p.127)**

Belief, intention, habit, creation

What you believe to be true is true. What you do not believe to be true is *not* true. Henry Ford said: "If you believe that you will succeed, you are right. If you believe that you will not succeed, you are also right."

Our beliefs provide the ingredients for our habits of perspective; how we perceive the world working.

Those repeated thoughts and feelings about how the world works lead to habitual actions.

All of these habitual thoughts, feelings and activities reinforce our original beliefs and create a picture of what is true. Since we have beliefs and habits of perception we tend to notice situations and other people that confirm these beliefs. Essentially we prove to ourselves that our perceptions are true.

For instance, a man who thinks women are simple minded or incompetent will tend to notice and remember situations in which women don't function well. He will tend to not notice or ignore when they do.

A woman who thinks men are always looking at her with sexual intentions will tend to notice the men that do, and hear comments as having sexual overtones. She will tend to ignore the ones that do not.

We are all creatures of belief and habit. Some times these beliefs and habits serve us well and sometimes they don't.

Our beliefs generate our perspectives and those perspectives generate thinking and feeling and behavior. Those behaviors become habitual and as we note the effects of those habits we can see a picture or a pattern of how our lives are. When we change the beliefs we also change the picture we expect to see, and so, life also changes.

Will grew up in a household with lots of love and also lots of dysfunction. He was given high ideals about being kind, generous and careful about his rights as a human being. He was taught that he had the right to speak what he believed, and to be respected and treated fairly regardless of his appearance and personal beliefs, and so long as he was not hurting anyone, the right to do as he liked. At the same time he was ignored and those very rights were also ignored. Since he had been taught to think one way and treated the opposite way, a conflict grew within him. There was a battle going on inside. His true inner self was constantly fighting to be acknowledged and valued all the while believing that it never would.

As a young adult he grew his hair into dreadlocks and grew marijuana commercially for a living. In the common terms of his culture his appearance and work broadcast a story of disrespect and disregard for himself and those around him (this disrespect matched the way he was treated as a child). The story he clung to included kindness, generosity and respect for humans while believing that he would never be treated that way: a constant battle within. Because of his appearance he was often harassed by police and arrested, sometimes for no justifiable reason. What became important to him was to constantly protest unfair treatment even though he lived a life of privilege and plenty. He created himself as a target. He actually lived the victim role because he believed that was the only avenue available. All of this while being financially quite successful.

He learned to believe that the world would treat him unfairly. Even though he was wealthy, generous and kind, he identified with those people who were habitually oppressed and found camaraderie in their common suffering. He believed in the inevitability of suffering and so created an appearance and lifestyle that matched his oppressed friends. His beliefs generated a picture of suffering and inability to create change or speak effectively for justice. He then painted himself into the picture.

At a young age, the conflict between his experiences and his beliefs turned inward. He developed Crones disease and his body attacked itself. The internal conflict manifested as a physical illness. His response was to do his best to manage the symptoms of his disease. In his case this meant smoking over a pound of marijuana per month which allowed him to digest food and have some physical comfort.

Will's thinking told him that fair treatment was not a reliable thing to expect in life. This generated a perspective that said, essentially, "there is nothing I can do to change this." What he then experienced in life were unfair situations. His belief in unfair treatment generated thoughts and feelings that matched those beliefs. Because he thought about it and had feelings about it regularly this perspective repeatedly brought him into contact with situations about himself and others that were of course unfair and hopeless.

His beliefs and perspective created his reality for him.

Will lived most of his life believing in a habit of thinking and behavior that said: *Though I value kind and loving treatment for myself and others, and I act on that belief, still, others in the world will not always treat me that way. I can expect to encounter injustice, and when I protest, it will not matter.* His pattern of belief repeatedly brought him back to protest, which produced no change.

Complaining about unfair treatment gave him a momentary feeling of relief and was, in the end, ineffective as a pathway to create change. The reality he created actually affirmed his belief in his own helplessness. He lived his days repeating a cycle of helpless protest on the outside, while his body battled itself on the inside.

Invite the Magic

Your magic is your unique ability to create or manifest or just notice and appreciate using your natural gifts, abilities and perspectives. Your style of magic is available to you now.

What brings you to this moment with energy and clarity? This is an indicator of the presence of your magic. An inspired idea. A hard days work. A kiss. Exercise. Being artistic. Listening to music. Smelling the roses. Helping someone heal. Dancing. Accomplishing a task… The list is endless.

You are in charge, now! This means that at this moment or at any moment you can tune in to the full ecstatic tingly radiant sensate *connected with everythingness* of this moment. This is the starting place of creation and appreciation and action. That is why all exercises start with "I am here." So take a breath, feel it on your lips as you exhale and notice. Notice your surroundings. Notice yourself inside. Notice in a new way. Notice more than you did before.

As you notice remember that this moment is always a starting place. It can be the start of a new thought, a new feeling or a whole new way of life for yourself or your family or your whole community. You can notice that you are happy or satisfied; sad or hurting; blessed and grateful; capable and powerful. You can simply slip into the warm ecstasy of connectedness in this moment with no thought at all.

Breathing with intention is actively inviting the magic that is always available to you to use. You can use it to manifest what you want. You can use it to simply come into the moment right now. It allows you to actively create your life as you want it to be now. It is *you* moving consciously into your beliefs, intention and power as a creator to affect yourself and all your relations – now.

> **Exercise: Inviting magic (G27 p.125)**
> **Exercise: Noticing my magic (C3 p.93)**

Your magic is your natural ability in this moment to notice and create your reality. Noticing your magic is the act of inviting yourself to be in the middle of that ability.

Think about the word "inspiration." It means "to breathe in." It also means being one with the creative or generative impulse of an idea or manifestation. Being "one with" means "immersed in" or "part of." It points at an exalted sense of drive, motivation, or desire to create or to reach a goal.

Purposeful breathing puts you in the middle of inspiration right now. You breathe in and when you combine that breath with intention you change your body, your perspective and emotions.

With regular purposeful breathing you purposely invite the magic of your ability to create into the now. You can bring your creative ability into action.

I have a regular practice of breathing for clarity and health. I breathe deeply and rapidly, for 3-4 minutes and do this twice in a row. If, as I do this I think of something I want, then pathways to accomplish what I want rise naturally in my mind. Some times I have to stop and write them down they come so quickly. Life is waiting patiently to give you what you want.

> **Exercise: Breathing for clarity (A4 p.84)**

Remember: sometimes *what you want* changes. Sometimes with loving attention and clarity what happens is that instead of wanting a certain thing or outcome, your point of view changes so that you move to a place of acceptance or even joy about what you have. That can actually be the change you want most.

Also as you go through the process of breathing with intention more and more, you will naturally begin to know yourself better and better. As you do you may find options and desires that you had not previously thought of. What a gift!!!

Inviting the magic that is always at hand means inviting change in the world. It also means inviting change inside of you.

Chapter 5

FROM A CERTAIN POINT OF VIEW

Consensus reality:
What we *all* agree is true

You can uncover your consensus reality by asking the question: What beliefs do I carry and perhaps act on each day that I think *everyone* agrees with? Here are some examples:

- If I work hard and sacrifice I will succeed.

- I am only worthy or valuable if I do certain things for myself or others or if I hold certain beliefs.

- I am superior or inferior to others because of my appearance, age, race, gender or abilities.

- I need to be independent, and not ask for help.

- I need to behave so that others approve.

- I am only valuable if I serve others.

- I am only valuable if I succeed a accumulating things.

- I cannot speak or live my truth in many situations.

- I am basically disconnected from others and my environment.

- Men and women operate with different rules.

The belief that *everyone* agrees about these ideas can keep you from questioning them. You are not alone! Others also think differently from the majority! Question these beliefs and rules!! Question them all!!

Breathe about them in inquiry!

What is true for you

> **Exercise: Questioning my thoughts or beliefs (C10 p.95)**

When you question existing beliefs you open the door to new possibilities. Inviting that new belief in for consideration and reevaluation is the first step to change; to living a more authentic life. For instance, I've heard it said that it is more blessed to give than to receive. I don't agree. I think there is plenty of blessing in all of it. Perhaps one could enjoy both equally.

Invite the truth in *your* terms.

> **Exercise: Identifying my true beliefs (C16 p.97)**

Limitless possibilities

Consider the idea that life will work for you in the way that you believe or know that it will work Also consider that you may be able to open up to new, unknown and limitless possibilities. When presented with a possibility that is too unusual, for most of us, the mind immediately steps in and says "I can't really do that because of "good" reasons or "sensible" limits. Most of these reasons have been taught, figured out or passed on to us.

Moving into new or unknown perspectives about what can happen may not feel easy, but can be the necessary ingredient bringing "limitless" into the range of possibility.

Some of our internal guidelines, and what we believe to be true, we may not have decided ourselves. These are carried perspectives. These influences can be carried forward from several sources without conscious knowledge.

- Parents' or caregivers' behavior or emotional attitudes that we act out without thinking

- Cultural beliefs or attitudes that *everyone* agrees with so we don't think to reconsider

- Ancestral influence in the form of beliefs or behavior that have been passed on for many generations and are no longer useful

- Past life incidents or traumas

- Childhood traumas or fears

As you invite limitless possibility, consider widening your view of what is true, not true or maybe true. The wider the view, the more that is possible.

> **Exercise: True, not true, maybe true (C12 p.96)**
> **Exercise: Releasing carried perspective (E3 p.105)**
> **Exercise: Allowing vision without limits (G9 p.119)**

Consider the role of a motivational speaker. She is there to invite you into a place of new beliefs and new possibilities. To help you generate a vision of what could be and then to step into that vision and allow it to be real. She always has success stories about new beliefs working for someone and creating wealth or personal fulfillment. And…she is always right. If you create a new vision and allow your beliefs to support that vision, your life will change.

Martin Luther King had a dream, a vision. Many people heard about it. They decided to step into that vision themselves and shift their beliefs to align with it. The culture began to change as a result. We now live in a different world. There are different rules, different beliefs and different *truths* about race and human equality in the U.S. than there were 50 years ago.

Easy or Difficult? How do you choose to learn?

I have heard that life will present you with the opportunity to learn. I believe this is true. I have also heard that life will give you increasingly blatant or painful situations to learn from if you refuse to pay attention. I think this is a matter of choice.

If you believe there is a prescribed path that you must follow and that somehow you are continuously being held up to a standard that you must reach to succeed, then this belief makes sense.

If you believe simply that achievement involves surmounting a series of difficulties then this also makes sense. Alternately if you believe life can be on-goingly gentle, perhaps you can learn and experience life that way.

What about plain joy? What about true loving presence? Do you need to somehow earn or pay for your joyous times? Perhaps you just deserve them anyway. Perhaps there are no requirements to have happiness or feel successful.

Life can be smooth. It can offer you what you want and need easily. As you grow to expect that life can and will provide for you, then it will. As you think and feel in terms of bounty and easiness and the generosity of your surroundings, then that is what you will begin to find.

> **Exercise: Life is easy (G20 p.123)**

What about anger or fear or sorrow? If we allow ourselves to feel them, these emotions can provide amazing opportunities to grow and expand, to see and feel new dimensions of the heart, to let grief or pain or anger help us express our passion or drive us to new thinking or help release old hurts and free the heart for growth and love.

Does hurt or anger or fear need to be permanently destructive or debilitating? I think not. If any of these lead you to feel out of control or helpless, perhaps those feelings need to be welcomed. Those out of control places actually can remove the thinking mind from the situation. With the "thinker" out of the way, we have the opportunity to feel, release and grow without limits. What an amazing opportunity.

Connect with another human being; Get witnessed. Get listened to and loved and cared for. Surely the out of control feelings will pass and you will be clearer after.

If life becomes intense will you still engage? Will you still stay here in the present? Your feelings and the direction they lead you will not really disappear. It will take a lot of your attention and energy to keep them away from yourself. If you manage to ignore them or forget about them, they will leak out randomly. Sometimes they leak out of you in emotional outbursts, sometimes unexplained behavior sometimes illness of the body or mind. If you don't engage now, then when will you? How much energy and attention will you expend avoiding what you feel.

It is often tempting to push away strong emotions that feel negative. They can seem overwhelming or dangerous to look at. It is important to know that if, instead of keeping them away, you invite them in – breathe them in – these emotions will often grow briefly and then subside quickly.

It takes a great deal of energy to keep a thought or feeling away from your self: to not think about or feel something. This alone can be exhausting and create a sense of overwhelm about a situation. Try inviting instead of avoiding. Get some attention and dive in. Welcome the feelings even if they are scary. In the end, identifying and welcoming these feelings *is* the easy way. Also, being witnessed as you welcome your emotion works better for most folks most of the time.

> **Exercise: Welcoming emotion (G11 p.120)**

Inquiry – What's really true for you now?

What's up? What's real? What's really true? What do I need? Is this thought or activity right for me? Can I trust my own thinking on this? Do I need help?

Sometime we simply don't know! We don't know what is right or what to choose or which way to turn. Sometimes it feels uncomfortable, or like we should know. Sometimes it's OK, or even funny.

So if you don't know, congratulations! You are in just the right place! Try an "Inquiry" exercise. There is a whole section of them ("Inquiry – Noticing What is Really True For Me" p. 89).

An outside opinion

As we are all creatures of habit, our thoughts and emotions and behaviors tend to be repeated without reconsideration each time. When it becomes obvious that a change is wanted , or we simply to find out what is true, it is often a good idea to get an outside opinion that can provide a safe and beneficial new idea or new behavior.

In conventional therapy we can access the inner child for this purpose or sometimes the higher power or the image of a trusted ally. We can also access the opinions of animal spirits, spirit guides, angels, gods or goddesses, deceased relatives, earth, air, fire, water, plants or even celestial bodies.

I often invite the opinion or protection of the bear spirit in my work with people. He is a big (ten feet tall) grizzly bear. His aspect is gentle, his opinions are strong and simple, and his strength is unchallengeable as a protector. I invite people to carry this image with them into the day. Bear is a strong ally for safety and change.

Here I introduce the All Knowing All Seeing self. You have one. I have one. We all have one.

The All Knowing All Seeing self is an aspect of you that knows all and sees all. The All Knowing All Seeing self is completely in touch with your conscious mind and also your unconscious mind, with God as you understand God, with everything necessary so that it can inform you accurately about any question you have about yourself.

So how do you get in touch with your All Knowing All Seeing self?

First, take a breath and accept the idea that the All Knowing All Seeing self is real and accessible to you now. Then, do these exercises:

Exercise: Welcoming the All Knowing All Seeing self (C1 p.92)
Exercise: Listening to the All Knowing All Seeing self (C6 p.94)

As you become familiar with you're All Knowing All Seeing self, do so with integrity. Look and listen carefully. Your All Knowing All Seeing self is impartial and always knows the truth. When talking to the All Knowing All Seeing self it is easy to identify the difference between truth and fear-based or habitual thinking. Stand in your personal integrity and take the time to notice this difference.

The point here is to relax and trust that if you are open, life will provide a good answer to your questions, and even perhaps one you had not thought of.

In the end there are no limits. You can start living as a powerful creator with all the support you want and need whenever you like.

Welcoming

What are you welcoming? Sometimes there is a belief or an intention or activity that we want to welcome. We want to invite newness or change or bring prosperity or passion or health into our lives. Purposely thinking about and consciously welcoming what you want is a powerful way to create intention and instigate change. Try making a list of what you want in positive terms. State what you want as though you already have it. Then breathe as you voice what you want.

Examples: Mix and match the following two columns to suit you personally or make up statements that fit you:

I have	life without fear
I am consciously inviting	more than enough money to meet my needs
I lovingly invite	supportive, loving relationships
I am allowing	a good job where I am appreciated
I am creating	$312.47 by next Tuesday
I expect	no attachments to other people opinions
I live in	peace inside me
I will have	no worries (worrying)
I welcome	time and attention from safe, loving people
I am	enough time to rest well
	internal ease about speaking my truth
	(your specific desire)

Remember that when you move into welcoming you are broadcasting a message to the universe inviting something new. You can include a lot of thought and emotion about how that new thing will happen. This can work well. It can also restrict the response the universe has for you. Another approach is to welcome newness in simple form and trust that life works and so will provide solutions. You may find that change or help comes from unexpected places.

For instance if you say to yourself "I have peace inside me" and then follow that thought with thoughts like. I can feel peaceful if I make more money or improve my relationship with my children or lose weight, you are including restrictions in your welcoming. Indeed, you will likely not feel peaceful until some or all of these conditions are met. If you simply take a breath and say "I have peace inside me" allowing yourself to move into peacefulness now, you are not including conditions. Your possibilities for success are much greater. You will likely experience peacefulness much more easily, and because you do experience peace you will also radiate that peace. The universe will notice and respond. Your body can relax. Your mind can lighten and perhaps someone will come by and smile or make a kind comment to you. Look to be affirmed! It happens all the time. Life is waiting to give you what you want. Believe it is true! It is!

Sometimes as we look towards newness we get stuck or scarred. An old belief, fear or habit stands in the way of movement. Also sometimes these old perspectives on life can have emotions, even difficult emotions attached to them. Consider the possibility of welcoming these too.

Welcoming difficult emotions

Difficult emotions can be scary or overwhelming and we often avoid them. Here's a trick!

It takes a great deal of energy and focus to keep feelings and fears away from yourself. It can be exhausting to maintain that energy output. So the trick is: if you welcome the difficult feelings and the thoughts that go with them, they will then tend to dissipate more quickly. Instead of shying away, breathe them in, experience the feelings. They may feel more intense for a while but then you will tend to release, relax, think better and move through more quickly. It will take a lot less effort in the long run. And, here's the magic! Your thinking will change. Your reasoning will change and your view on behavior will change with it. You are giving yourself the opportunity to welcome newness, in other words, to get what you want.

Because the load of unexpressed emotion often generates fear and internal restriction (both sometimes unacknowledged), it also generates ineffective and inaccurate thinking. This thinking changes belief and resultant behavior.

Beverly was a 43 year old woman, a successful attorney, happily married and about 100 lbs overweight. She enjoyed respect and success at work, a lively social life and a good relationship with her husband including lots of sex.

When asked about the extra weight she carried she admitted that it served as a protective barrier so men would not notice her as a sexually attractive woman and that she had been raped in her mid twenties. She also said she had a high sex drive, sometimes wanting sexual contact 10 times in a day, and sometimes felt that she could not get enough. It did not satisfy her for long.

She said she had faced the feelings around her rape successfully as evidenced by her ease and welcome of frequent sexual contact. Mentioning the rape again later she got uncomfortable, asking that we switch to some other topic.

Eventually she identified the area around her womb as often feeling cold or like she was absent from that area. Looking further, though it was uncomfortable, she opened up to release more feelings around her rape and even further back to feeling unseen and never good enough to please her father. She said it felt like she had been holding on to this frozen place in her womb since she was about 5 and trying to get it thawed out by being finally, fully welcome…by a man.

Medically she was healthy and fertile, but she and her husband had tried to become pregnant for 6 years without success.

Her rape had been horrible, but she was determined to recover her sense of safety around sex and did. Though she did feel safe being sexual, even repeated contact with many orgasms did not thaw out that frozen feeling for long or allow her to be fully present in her own body. Sexual climax gave her a brief sense of warmth and loving connection that did not fill up her heart and did not last. Her desire became addictive. She was grasping for a fleeting sense of connection through sex as many men do.

Finding a broad basis for self value was confusing. Her professional success allowed her to stand in confidence and move in a powerful way which was very affirming. Personally, the face of her marriage and her social and sex life looked right, but felt empty. Even with apparent proof of her success and value, the little voice in her head continually doubted that it was true.

Over time, further attention to the uncomfortable feelings about her rape and her father's indifference freed her thinking and changed her view of herself. Each time she opened herself to that frozen place, her first reaction was fear, but then increasing warmth and with it memories returned and she began to feel more seen, accepted and valuable. Her sense of desperation about being loved and wanted diminished, and her sexual contact became more fulfilling. More and more she felt as though she was solidly in her body and in her heart…all of it. She easily lost weight. Breathing exercises helped her welcome herself back into her own body and change what the little voice in her head was saying.

Exercise: Safety while feeling emotion (G12 p.120)

It is often best, or even necessary to get some loving attention while welcoming difficult or scary feelings. Find someone that is safe, that you trust to talk to, such as a friend or therapist.

Remember that it is unlikely that you are the only one who has ever felt this way

Remember that the person you choose to talk to is not you, and therefore does not carry the same fears or difficulties that you do. This difference is often enough to help create a feeling of safety so you can make a time and place in safety to have your big feelings.

It is tempting in this culture to hide or isolate when times are fearful or sad or overwhelming. The dominant cultural norm teaches us to stay isolated from others in the mistaken belief that we will somehow lose their love or respect or lose our personal value by asking for help. Most of us will freely offer loving attention to a child when they are hurt or overwhelmed or need support.

Remember, you are no less valuable and deserving of loving attention than a child. As you look for support and attention, take good care of your self. Do your best to choose someone to talk to who will listen without trying to fix you, who will keep what you say confidential, and with whom you feel safe.

Chapter 6

SHIFTING A HABIT

When you come to a place where you recognize the need for a change and it is time to shift a habit or, more accurately, to create a new habit that serves you better, consider the following:

Take the time for yourself to sit and answer these questions. Write down the answers.

- What keeps happening in your life that you want to be different?

- What would you like your life to be or feel like instead? (Create a vision. Give yourself time to dream.) Try this exercise:

> **Exercise: Creating a vision (G8 p.119)**

- What do you feel or think or do repeatedly that creates the old thinking or behavior habit? Keep it simple. Avoid negative self criticism. *You may not know how you are at cause without blame.* If you don't know or simply want to confirm your answer to this question try:

> **Exercise: How am I at cause? (C12 p.96)**

- What would you like to feel or think or do instead? Refer to your vision and notice the ingredients to your change. This can be an easy question to answer. If it is, try:

> **Exercise: Choosing a new habit (F18 p.115)**
> **Exercise: Welcoming new perspective. (G3 p.117)**
> **Exercise: My body (heart or spirit) has the answer (C15 p.97)**

- If it is not easy to identify what you want, try an Inquiry Exercise or try:

> **Exercise: Identifying the change I truly want (C9 p.95)**

- What are manageable steps toward this change? Be real with yourself. Set goals that you can realistically accomplish so you can succeed.

- Use suggestions from *Making It Real* (Chapter 8) to notice, support and celebrate your progress.

About change or shifting your life perspective

Simpleness: I believe that for most of us, in the end, changes and revelations and learnings are simple. Sometimes the new direction is obvious and sometimes we hide it from ourselves. It may be that we believe we need long and complex pathways involving great effort and emotion to have change. Perhaps we believe we have to earn the right to have a change. Perhaps we believe we need to accomplish each step along the way fully to have change. These beliefs can work well, but do we really need them?

I have found that people who carry fear or are stuck about past or ongoing experiences need to release the stuckness they carry in their body or heart or mind to be able to allow change. This may involve lots of time and emotion and complexity, and it may not.

Alternately you may simply have habitual beliefs, or even beliefs that you think *everyone* agrees with, that guide, or limit your behavior.

For instance most people believe they need to work hard and pay their dues in time and effort in order to succeed. Is this really true?

These beliefs may no longer be useful to you. Therefore you are available for change or new decisions about what is true for you now, perhaps without great effort or emotion.

Leah was born a gentle and loving girl. The family she grew up in was entrenched in religion based forms of fear, shame and competition for self esteem and self value. Her sisters competed with her for attention from her parents and from boys to the point of cruelty, and her brothers terrorized her. Even though she was exposed to the rules and forms of their efforts to compete for attention, still she could never enter effectively into this way of relating to other people. She could not shame or dominate or hurt another in order to feel better or feel valuable.

She grew up believing that her best alternative to her family's model of behavior was to serve others in an attempt to be loved and valued. Still, there was something missing in the story she told herself. She had never experienced being loved and valued just for herself and so didn't really believe that this would ever happen no matter what she did. Of course, because she believed this, she was right. It didn't work.

The internal story she carried, taught to her by her family, about what to expect from close relationships had led her to a husband who, though kind, dominated her and was unable to fully value her wisdom and gentle demeanor, or to honor the power of her loving presence.

With her children, though she had effectively modeled gentleness and loving, she also believed that saying "no" or making limits for them was being mean, and so had not shown them the loving strength of her voice and opinion by insisting on healthy limits.

When I met her she was exhausted with her efforts over her whole life to serve others and trying to feel loved and accepted. It had not worked. The elasticity of her youth was fading and her energy was drained. She was done with that way of surviving. She also didn't really know that there was an alternative. Her beliefs and habits about feeling small and powerless had been reinforced all her life.

We talked about a different point of view. One where her love based perspective about life was supremely important and she was naturally valuable no matter what. A perspective where her opinions were as valuable as anyone (including men) and she could begin to reclaim her voice.

We involved her body in this new perspective and change with energy realignment, spiritual cleansing and purposeful breathing. She opened to this new possibility in a few hours and her life changed.

Later, we involved her mind and heart in supporting this change with visualization, coaching and 7 breaths exercises to literally rewire the new perspective into her body and thoughts. We invited her to shift her beliefs about how to express her loving power and therefore the new ways she could expect to be treated by others.

I invite you to consider the idea that the change you want is available now. The life you want and the feeling state you want and the abundant joy is here. Pick an exercise or a few. Start doing them every day and start inviting the change. You may be surprised at how easy and effective it is. If you make the decision to invite change and invite a perspective that serves you better, your old habits and resistances may come up for review. *You can often choose a new perspective simply by making the decision to do so.*

If the voice in your head says "I haven't done this before," or "I can't do this" you can answer it by deciding "Even so, I *am* going to do it now."

If you meet resistance or refusal from yourself, you may need to release ideas or emotions or tightness in the body in order to fully embrace a new direction. It is usually best to get some loving attention to help with these releases. Talk to someone you trust as you shift an idea. Spend time with a safe friend or therapist or mentor to help you release emotions or become open to change. Get some effective body work or do some physical exercise to release tension in the body. Get some help looking into the subconscious mind or into past lives to find out about unexplained fears or resistance or blank places in your thinking and reactions. Acknowledge and release these. You will then be more open to change.

Noticing patterns outside of us

Patterns are all around you. They all work. Astrology, traffic noise, numerology, tea leaves, laboratory blood tests, signs of coming weather, iridology, body language, animal movements, red and green traffic lights, EKGs, palmistry, road maps, etc., etc.

The point is that we are all connected and that because of that connection, the thoughts, intentions and movements we create as we live life effect everything around us. That effect creates patterns and signs. These patterns can be noticed and understood and responded to.

The ones that you are used to noticing and believing and perhaps those that you think are universally accepted are no more or less real than those patterns that are unknown or unproven to you.

Some of these patterns seem physical or 5 sensory and some seem etheric. A road map for instance is a visual pattern that we look at to find information or direction. We rely on it to inform us as to which way to go to get to our destination. Watching the movement of a hawk as it flys by can be equally informative, but most of us are unused to reading signs and meanings from the movement of a hawk. Astrology is a pattern that some of us have learned to interpret and believe in. It has become believable and reliable for many of us.

The universe is always available to show you what is true; to show you what is true for you, or what was true or what is about to be true for you or for others.

There is always a message available for you. The message is usually present and appropriate. Have you ever noticed how often the message from a fortune cookie is accurate or very close to accurate? Loving connection and guidance is everywhere and it is actually easy to see.

Want to learn something new or get an opinion about something or about yourself? Want a direction to move or to see what is important? Want to ask a question of the universe? Pick a tarot card. Open a good book and read where your eyes land. Notice the movements of animals around you. Start paying attention to your gut response to life. Start trusting your Intuition. You are a connected active part of your environment and your environment works well with you in it. It will flow with you and around you and it will announce its direction and intentions just as you do to it. You can see and sense what is true any time you like. Invite it. It is available to you.

This is an awareness that we all have. Most of us have been trained or conditioned to ignore it. It can be easily reclaimed.

Exercise: Noticing signs in my environment (C4 p.93)

Learn to pay attention in a new way. Breathe deep, relax, allow your mind to clear and simply notice what is around you from an open and welcome point of view. Physical things and also thoughts and feelings. The message you receive may not be distinct or definite like "your shoe is untied." It may be more of a feeling or sense about what is true for you that you didn't notice before you cleared a place to notice. As you do this more and more often you will become more sensitive, more aware and more accurate.

Exercise: Accepting the love all around me (G18 p.122)
Exercise: Paying attention (C5 p.93)

As you invite new perception be careful about tuning in to fear, habitual fear or superstition. These cloud your connection to your highest and best pathway to joy and success.

Noticing Patterns inside of us

Look around you. There are patterns everywhere. Patterns inside and outside of you. Patterns in the sky, the water, the earth, the wind. Patterns in your thinking, feeling and behavior. There are also patterns that are used to identify you or what is going on for you or sometimes what will go on for you. Doctors and healers look for patterns of the body mind and the spirit to see you more fully and help you identify what is going on and to help you change and heal.

In relationships we often show our patterns of thinking and behavior to the people we connect with so they learn what to expect from us.

There are patterns in our reactions to life situations. Habits and patterned reactions to familiar situations allow us to think less and focus less in the present. We react (do, think, speak, feel) in a patterned way and the result is usually satisfactory. Humans tend to be creatures of habit. We look for patterns in our daily experiences. If we are presented with a familiar set of circumstances we will tend to reach into our life experience to find a patterned or habitual response rather than reassess each situation and then create a new response each time. Most of the time this serves us well. It would be exhausting to pay that much attention to every situation in life. Imagine reassessing and redeciding what to do each time you see a green or red light while driving or reevaluating how to tie your shoes each morning.

What do you do when someone laughs or hugs you? Some of these reactions are desirable What do you do when someone cries, or cuts you off at an intersection? Some reactions do not serve our highest and best interest or that of our relations.

If some one hugs you, you may open your heart and body and drink in the touch as a wonderful affirmation of connection and love. You may also become stiff and fearful, or feel ashamed. There are also many other possible reactions. What do you choose?

If someone cries, you may feel irritable and impatient and want to quiet them immediately. You may also interpret it as a signal that someone needs help and an invitation to give some love or attention. There are also many other possible reactions. What do you choose?

Look at your habits and patterns. Pick one you would like to change. Find a *Seven Breaths* exercise that moves you close to the change you want, or alter an exercise to be just right for you.

Seven Breaths is a simple, powerful road to the shift in perspective that you want.

It is often difficult to simply stop doing or thinking or reacting a certain way. It is easier to start doing something else. This moves you toward a new habit, a way that will serve you better, and create the results you want.

> **Exercise: Choosing a new habit (F18 p.115)**

Affirmation

Affirmations work. Affirming what you know or know to be true or want to be true speaks to your subconscious mind and helps shift your belief, therefore your intentions and behavior. Doing this while purposefully breathing works better. Some of this happens on the conscious level and some on the unconscious level. Consciously you may invite the new habit of thinking positive thoughts or making desirable conclusions about a part of your world view. This informs your subconscious and will begin to change your perspective and your behavior.

Your beliefs and perspectives are written into and stored in your body as energetic patterns that you create and sustain through attention or of lack of attention. Your mind, heart and body hold the active template or guiding pattern for your reality. These patterns stored in your body are linked unconsciously to how you perceive reality. These energetic patterns can then come back to you from your body and subconscious in the form of thoughts and habits that generate your behavior and reactions to recognizable situations.

As you repeatedly affirm the new direction you want to move in or the intention you want to engage in, you actually change your body's energetic signature and it's physical state.

Breathing is a physical act. Breathing with intention involves your body actively in the change you are inviting. Breathing with intention moves energy in your body and changes your body to a new frequency. Your energetic signature shifts. This allows more direct accessibility to change for you. You are literally rewriting the active template for your reality and therefore what you will think and how you will behave and be treated.

Yes…also how you will be treated! The energy signature of your body and what that means about your beliefs radiates from you. Others can tell and will tend to treat you in accordance with what you believe is true about yourself.

> **Exercise: I am treated well (G19 p.123)**

So any form of affirmation of who you are or what you want is helpful. Involving your body on purpose (breathing with intention or doing a 7 breaths exercise) will be more effective.

Learning and practice: How the brain works

Basically the brain learns one thing at a time and works best when it is clearly being asked to learn only one thing. Like a computer it takes one bit of input at a time.

The brain is a complex mechanism, and so unlike a computer, that one thing that the brain can learn can be complex.

For a human, something that is complex like an idea or a behavior or an emotional pattern is composed of one or perhaps many pieces of known input experienced over time. If a large part of what someone is learning is made of information that is already known, then that information is part of a whole picture that is still recognized by the brain as one new thing

Being complex and human we also have other capacities. One of those capacities is to learn one thing at a time and then quickly learn another. It may seem like we are learning many things at once. Another is memory. Things to learn can be called up from memory and can be learned one at a time.

So we can learn one thing at a time, we can learn one thing that is connected to many known things. We can learn one thing and then another very quickly and we can call up memories to integrate into our learning.

Still, the brain prefers learning at its simplest.

The most effective way to learn is to purposely go after one new thing at a time and if that one thing is too big, then to slow down, identify its component parts, and then learn each of the parts one at a time so that they are easy to learn. In the end this is the quickest way to learn. Trying to take in too much at one time can result in mistakes which have to be unlearned. This is a more complex and time consuming process.

This book gives simple ideas to learn, one at a time. Still, for you, at any given time it may be easier to focus on one instead of seven at one sitting. Please do what you sense is best for you. One idea at a time is enough!

Chapter 7

INVITING YOU TO THRIVE

If you can stay balanced, healthy and in the present, your experience of life will be the best. You will thrive.

Balanced and healthy means engaging in activity and connection that feeds you and supports your authentic self, and also recharging when you are depleted.

In the present means allowing your perception to be here now and your involvement in life to start here and now. This is different from simply reacting from old patterns or missing what is happening in front of you.

Staying balanced means there is a majority of your time spent engaged in activity or in a state of being that you find truly acceptable, satisfying or engaging in your own terms. For instance many people work at a job that meets financial needs or their beliefs about staying busy, and also know that the job does not feed them internally. It does not add to their sense of fulfillment or radiance.

Staying balanced also means that when life becomes overwhelming you take the time and attention required to move back to a state of ease, calm and balance; you seek out nurturing, relaxation, and release.

Staying Healthy

Staying healthy means that what you take into your body, mind and heart gives you more than it takes away. It feeds you more than it depletes you. There are three aspects of this. Choosing that which is feeding, avoiding that which can pollute you, and clearing or cleansing.

Choosing what feeds you includes eating well and moderately, exercising appropriately and engaging with life, nature and people in a way that adds to your sense of well being. Finding a way to engage in life's tasks that is uplifting. Knowing how much to rest and play and sleep to recharge yourself.

Avoiding pollution is a function of self knowledge and knowledge of your environment. Knowing what foods, air, light, and weather your body reacts to poorly. Knowing if the air you breathe and the water you drink is clean, and if your environment is free from poisons. Identifying the people or social situations that take too much energy away from you. Knowing and sticking to your own limits so you do not engage in too much stress or overwhelm.I find, for instance, that sugar is poison for my body, also that overcast or fluorescent light drains my energy, and that I need to avoid people who demand a lot of emotional attention without asking for it.

Clearing or cleansing is knowing what works best for you when you take in something that is distressing in some way so you have a way to let go of it – talk, exercise, massage, yoga, shaking, vocalizing, crying, energy work, sleep, vitamins, rest, play, expressing your emotion, yawning, etc.

Your body is like a journal of your life. Everything that you go through is written in your body as you go through it. Sometimes it is written in memories, sometimes in conscious or unconscious energy and behavior patterns that you can either release or hold on to. Patterns of belief about what we are supposed to keep can create retention. If you retain enough of this energy that does not match your inherent self (trauma, fear, overwhelm, grief, emotion), it can make you sick.

Samantha, a 44 year old married mother of six and a non-drinker of alcohol was second on the list in California for a transplant with a failing liver. Her early treatment as a child and later as a wife left her with the belief that in order to be successful as a loving being, it was her job to carry or filter all of the emotions of the people around her that she loved. She did this for all of her children, her mother and her husband and friends. Her belief was that it was her obligation to give away her life force so that others might feel good or balanced.

The liver is a major filter in the body. It filters out toxic or unhealthy elements from the blood for disposal. It is also an energetic and emotional filter. As Samantha carried more and more of the fears and difficulties of those around her without releasing them, her liver deteriorated. She was dying.

As she became conscious of her need to stop carrying or filtering other people's emotions, she began to also change the character of her relationships. She learned to say "no" to listening to the accusations and anger of her mother. She refused to take the blame for her husband's fears and infidelities and after a few months she left him. She began to insist on respectful behavior from her children. She changed her diet to more healthy food. She stepped into belief of herself as a lovingly powerful being and into her natural gifts as a healer without holding on to other people's fears and doubts.

After several months her liver began to improve and after 10 months she came off the transplant list. After 14 months her liver was functioning within normal limits. As she reclaimed her personal balance and stopped processing other people's emotions her illness also improved.

To stay healthy you need to pay attention to self care. Your body needs enough rest, exercise, touch, nutritious food, and to not be polluted. Your heart needs loving connection however you conceive of it. Your mind needs gainful employment, i.e. something to do or be that is satisfying to you so you can be and feel successful. This can include reducing the amount of thinking you do.

Being in the present means that you regularly are paying enough attention to what is going on right now to see or feel what is here now or what is happening. So, whether you like what you see or not, you are noticing! It also means that you are being here from your true self. In other words the thoughts you think and the behavior you display come from your real self as opposed to beliefs or patterns that you have adopted from others that do not resonate truly with you.

This is also the place in life from which you can access magic. From the present place and moment all is possible. This is part of the magic of the shaman. When you are fully here now you can most easily access your power as a creator.

Ingredients to balanced, healthy, and in the Present

Rest, meditation or renewal, emotional discharge, being heard, connection, creativity, ecstasy, touch, love, sex, sensation, self acceptance, engaging in satisfying activity, knowing my life purpose, knowing myself, recognizing my inherent nature and natural gifts, how I work best, what makes up a supportive environment, feeding myself in my own terms, what I really like, exercise, staying flexible physically and emotionally, eating well, nutrition, emotional comfort, keeping tabs on the little voice in my head, knowing how to get along without stress or worry, processing difficulties or retentions, taking the time to be here, watching for over busy-ness, engaging in ritual or reminders of your connection to all life. Pick one of these ingredients and invite it into your life this week or put it into the following exercise.

> **Exercise: Stepping into change now (F21 p.116)**

Calling you forth

What calls you forth? What piques your interest; sparks your curiosity? What fires you up? What calls to your values and gifts and desires? What stimulates you into action or movement or ecstasy? What generates creativity? What beckons to your mind and heart? What can you feel in your body? What flushes your face or sends shivers up your spine? What gives you that long solid warm sense of satisfaction?

What connection with a person or group of people? What vision in your mind or memory from your life? What loving moment? What painful moment? What sensory delight? What memory of accomplishment? What ritual or celebration? What difficult ordeal? What ecstatic or expanded state of being? What fear?

Do you think about or pay attention to what calls you forth? Are you satisfied accepting what the culture or other people believe is valuable and then living life on those terms? Are you OK acting and reacting to what you are offered? Or... Do you want to want to experience your days knowing that your thoughts feelings and activities are created based on your real values and desires? Do you want to step into that choice?

I believe we always have the opportunity to thrive and to succeed. To engage in life with a high degree of expectation and to have that expectation met. So, we have the opportunity to have interesting stimulating, satisfying, fun and learning experiences. Maybe those experiences are actually the whole point of being here. If you take away the judgment about what has been good or bad in your life, haven't your experiences been amazing and fascinating, or at least interesting? Something to feel. Something to find or accomplish or have. Something to learn to do, or not to do; to be, or not to be (to coin a phrase).

Getting stuck in the perspective that some experiences are bad, and need to be blocked out or denied works well if you are looking for the experience or drama of going in and out of constriction or frozenness. It can also make you sick or fearful; more fascinating experience!

Look at the opportunity we get to play and to experience and test and learn and think and feel. What a gift this life is.

So what do you choose? What calls you forth in this moment and this lifetime? What experiences do you choose? Do you hear a call? Will you respond? If not now then when?

> **Exercise: Hearing life's call (F16 p.114)**
> **Exercise: Responding to life's call (F17 p.114)**

Your true life purpose or perspective

What is your true individual unique nature? What is your specific flavor or style as a human? Not what parents or your community or religion tell you, or even what humans in general are here for. Just you. This is the amazing totally unique perspective on life that is yours only. The one that includes all your gifts, true values and passions. When you're rooted in this point of view, and guiding your life from here, the work you do comes alive, the people you connect with are just the ones you need and want. Life is fulfilling – even joyous. You are balanced and powerful.

Are there some ideas or accomplishments that you were taught to value that don't seem real to you or to match your inner truth? When you take these away, what is left?

Each of us has a unique perspective, an individual way of being here. I have helped hundreds of people identify that perspective and no two have been the same. Knowing your life purpose gives you a useful and powerful piece of self knowledge. Working with that perspective gives rise to passionate activity, inspired creation and deeply satisfying tasks and relationships. It allows your life and moments to feel magical and fulfilling.

It helps inform you about why some endeavors and people have worked well for you and others have not. More importantly it will help you decide ahead of time about future career choices, relationships and pastimes.

If this process interests you, please contact me. Together we can uncover your unique life purpose in less than two hours in person or over the phone.

Chapter 8

MAKING IT REAL

As you shift your beliefs, perspective and behavior it is good to have reminders of the newness around you. Reminders and rituals support and solidify the changes we are inviting. We can invite and create change by practicing the new point of view we have chosen. Here are a few suggestions:

- Find a small object that can be carried in the pocket or purse that reminds you to think of your change or new perspective.

- Look at your own eyes in the mirror several times a day and speak your new beliefs to yourself.

- Talk to a safe friend regularly affirming your choice and your steps toward change.

- Fill a dropper bottle with clean water, hold it in your hand and speak your new belief out loud to instill the water with your intention. Label the bottle with your intention. Take a few drops under your tongue several times a day to affirm your new intention.

- Breathe on purpose and speak your new belief to yourself randomly during the day.

- Post notes in your environment (home, car, work) that state simply your new direction or desire.

- Create a work of art that represents your vision or change.

- Identify and write down the signs that tell you your life is changing and notice them.

- Make a *creation container* (box or bowl etc.) that holds writings and objects which represent your new beliefs and changes.

- Celebrate your progress! Allow yourself to feel proud and if appropriate, share your pride with someone safe.

- Create a ritual or ceremony that identifies and honors your true nature, wants and accomplishments. If appropriate, share it with someone safe.

- If there are fears coming up, find a safe time to welcome these difficult emotions so you can move through them to clearer thinking, feeling and behavior.

- Call yourself and leave a message stating your change so you can hear it later in your own voice.

- Remind yourself that you have all the time, ability and support you need to make your change. Then, do a "Breathing Exercise" to reinforce your change.

- Remember that you are loved now and always, no matter what.

- Remember that it is OK to make mistakes. Mistakes are sacred and important ingredients of your blessed journey as a human.

- Connect regularly with an ally – a safe person – the vision of a loving relative, animal spirit or wise teacher, your All Knowing All Seeing self or God.

- Do a *Seven Breaths* exercise twice a day.

Chapter 9

IF YOU GET STUCK

What is Stuck?

Sometimes it seems difficult or perhaps impossible to answer certain questions like:

- What do I want?
- Why can't I seem to embrace this change?
- Why can't I remember this part of my history?
- Why can't I ask for help?
- Why does this seem so hard?
- What is in the way of moving forward?
- Why am I afraid?
- Why am I so affected by another person's opinion?
- Where does this fear come from?
- Why do I hang on to this destructive pattern?
- Why do I feel so helpless or hopeless?
- Why do I go numb or blank?
- What do I need?
- What is normal or best for me in this situation?

Being available for change or shift

Sometimes when life feels out of balance or just wrong and it's time to change, you just can't get there. You can't move into the change. Maybe you see that change is at hand and maybe you have even been able to identify what change you want and see that it is a good direction to go, and still you can't seem to embrace motion toward it. So what's up?

First, check in with yourself. Ask if it is truly OK to allow this change at this time. Check with your mind, your feelings and your body to see what's really true. Trust yourself. Sometimes the answer is simply No. There may be a reason and there may not. Honor the answer you get with or without a reason.

Also, there are times when the answer is no and there seems no way to shift. There can be many reasons for this. I will address two: carried beliefs and vows.

Both carried beliefs and vows can be fully functional in the subconscious and unknown. They can therefore direct your thinking, feeling and behavior. This unconscious directive can resist change, and can also be shifted.

Vows are promises that you make to yourself or to others. For instance a parent may promise himself not to rest until his children are raised, so if you ask that parent if he is willing to take a vacation he will say no even knowing that he needs one. A nun may take a vow of poverty so that she will automatically refuse to accept the gift of ease or comfort provided by financial abundance.

Carried beliefs are beliefs we decide to adopt that come from other sources. The most common are generational and cultural. Generational beliefs are those we adopt from our parents or their parents or ancestors. These beliefs can be actual values or directives we remember being told to us by a parent, or they can simply be learned by watching the behavior of parents or caregivers. Cultural beliefs are told and modeled for us by family and a majority of people in our community. Since most people we know seem to agree about this thinking or behavior, we tend to accept them as true. These carried beliefs seem "true" and, although they may not actually match our personal values, we can use them as directing influences all of our lives.

Further, carried beliefs and vows can come from the influence of our ancestors or incidents in other lifetimes, making them difficult or impossible to access in memory.

> **Exercise: Is this really mine? (C26 p.100)**

If when you check in with your feelings you sense fear, ask yourself this question: If I were not afraid, would I be available for this change? If the answer is yes, try stepping into the fear briefly to move through it and breathe through it.

> **Exercise: Bane of fear (D1 p.101) or Moving through... (D5 p.102)**
> **Exercise: Identifying a fear (C2 p.92)**

Also, you can talk about it with someone safe.

What to do when you get stuck

What if you get stuck in fearful thinking or a habit you can't seen to shake, a relationship dynamic you keep cycling through, an addiction, or you have blank places in your memory or feelings of hopelessness, or powerlessness or failure, or depression or you can't seem to succeed, or to find out what you want or can't separate yourself from other people's opinions?

- Take a breath, slow down and pay attention. Pay loving attention to yourself. Be kind and accepting of yourself no matter how you feel or how you judge yourself. You always deserve this no matter what you think or feel. Pick any *Release* exercise, or:

> **Exercise: Releasing stuckness (E4 p.105)**

- Get some help from someone you feel safe with. What ever you may have been taught to believe, you deserve help and help is at hand. Always. Ask for input or attention from a friend, a therapist, your higher power, god, or spirit guides.

- Look and listen to your environment without judgment: the "random" comment from a passerby, the words of a child. Flip through a favorite book, stop randomly and read. Flip through this book. Read a passage. Notice how it speaks to you.

> **Exercise: Noticing signs in my environment (C4 p.93)**

- Do a *Seven Breaths* inquiry exercise. It can speak directly to what is going on with you.

- Notice the movement of a bird or animal and let it speak to you for direction or change.

- Life is immense. There is energy everywhere and guidance everywhere available for you!!!

- Move to the moment now. Close your eyes and breathe and forgive yourself for everything. I mean everything!

> **Exercise: Forgiving myself (H5 p.129)**

- After forgiving yourself, allow yourself the opportunity to be in this moment now enough to notice that there are possibilities for growth movement and change that you may not have considered or noticed.

- Remember that the little voice in your head will often speak to you from a narrow point of view driven by habit and outdated beliefs. You can choose not to believe it. If you find it difficult to allow the shift away from believing all of your own thoughts, get some help or attention.

> **Exercise: Moving through stuckness (D4 p.102)**
> **Exercise: Quieting the little voice (G10 p.120)**

- Get someone to lead you into a past life regression or ancestral clearing looking for your resistance or stuck place where there is no story.

- Avoid the mind. Get some clearing from physical movement, body work, spiritual clearing, energy clearing, dietary purging, or physical cleansing.

- Take it easy. Give yourself permission to learn and grow gently and slowly. You have all the time you need. You deserve this consideration.

The idea here is to live in the moment, have rich experiences and keep getting to know yourself better all the time. Sometimes knowledge of self needs a bit of help from the outside.

Conscious and Unconscious

You can talk, figure things out, look at your history and your reactions to situations. You can create new thinking, beliefs or habits.

That's the thinking conscious part. Your conscious mind learns and decides and believes and informs your subconscious mind about what is true. Your subconscious mind then believes it without question.

There's another part – your unconscious or subconscious mind. We figure things out mostly in the conscious mind. But most of our behavior patterning and reaction comes from the unconscious mind. Since it is unconscious, it is sometimes hard to identify what your thinking or behavior patterns are.

To make a change you often need to reeducate or redirect the unconscious mind through experience or repetition: Affirmations, *Seven Breaths* exercises, allowing priority to a new outside point of view, spiritual epiphany, healing, painful experiences, new perspective during dream time, life threatening experiences. How will you accept newness?

Outside help is very valuable. Other people see patterns and behavior in a light that we often do not see.

So here are some ways to get some help. Sharing your story with a safe friend or family member (remember to pick someone you truly feel safe with and ask for confidentiality if you want it), talk therapy, discharge therapy, life coaching, effective body work, massage, chiropractic, acupuncture, reiki, polarity, energy balancing, hypnosis, shamanic journey to connect with spirit guides or past life regression or shamanic clearing, soul retrieval, karmic clearing, subconscious clearing, Listening to your higher power or spirit guides, *Seven Breaths* and then sharing the results. Pick one that works for you.

> **Exercise: Listening to divine guidance (C7 p.94)**
> **Exercise: Welcoming my intuition (F7 p.111)**

Most of us are not taught, (or are taught not) to listen to natural voices: water, earth, wind, fire, animals that show up in front of you, and the natural voices of spirit. When you are upset or fearful or stuck in a destructive pattern, it is easy to "hear" the voice of habitual emotional response or fear based thinking or superstition (superstition is fear based conditional reality, i.e., if I do certain activities I will be OK and if I don't, life will punish me). These actually don't serve you well. Be careful. Remember that these reactions can seem useful and right, especially when other people agree with the reaction or behavior. In the end the test for *rightness for you* is to answer the questions:

- Does this behavior or solution really serve me well in the long run?

- Does it best serve everyone involved?

- Did it serve us all well when I did it last time?

Sometimes your habits and your thinking about your habits seem so right and normal that it doesn't occur to you what difference in thinking, belief or new behavior will spell success. Sometimes you are stuck and know you are stuck and don't know what to do next. Sometimes you are simply overwhelmed or confused and don't recognize that you are stuck. Look for a new, outside point of view. Get some help. Find a safe friend or a therapist or mentor to talk to.

Exercise: Moving through stuckness (D4 p.102)

BREATHING EXERCISES

A. CONSCIOUS BREATHING

(A1) Breathing for health, healing, and clarity
Sit comfortably, loosen clothing and time yourself.
1 – I am all here now
2 – Breathe faster and deeper than you normally do for 4-5 minutes

(A2) Breathing deeper
3 – I am here now
4 – I am completely connected to all that is
5 – I am breathing deeper
6 – I notice how this feels different
7 – As I breathe, my body welcomes this new feeling
8 – I will continue to breathe deeper (after this exercise) without needing to think about it
9 – Thank you for everything

(A3) Breathing for physical health
1 – I am here now
2 – I am completely connected to all that is
3 – As I breathe, my body relaxes
4 – I feel strong energy flow
5 – I send radiant energy to any unhealthy place
6 – I am functioning better
7 – Thank you for everything

(A4) Breathing for clarity

1 – I am here now
2 – I am completely connected to all that is
3 – As I breathe, my perceptions clear
4 – I have no need to think
5 – My body (heart, mind) is clear and relaxed
6 – I have the energy I need (or I know the path I need to take)
7 – Thank you for everything

(A5) Breathing for alertness

1 – I am here now
2 – I am completely connected to all that is
3 – As I breathe, my mind awakens
4 – As I breathe, my body is alert
5 – I have abundant energy
6 – I am fully present
7 – Thank you for everything

(A6) Breathing into the present

1 – I am here now
2 – I am completely connected to all that is
3 – I easily notice all that is in me
4 – I easily notice all that is around me
5 – I fully sense this moment
6 – Here I am
7 – Thank you for everything

B. AFFIRMING YOUR TRUE NATURE

(B1) Charlie's song
1 – I am here now
2 – I am unalterably connected to all that is
3 – The substance of that connection is unconditional love
4 – There are no limits to what is possible
5 – Love is me (…fills me …heals me …guides me)
   (pick one or more)
6 – I am loved
7 – Thank you for everything

(B2) Love
1 – I am here now
2 – I am completely connected to all that is
3 – I know love (I see love)
4 – Love fills me (There is more than enough love for me)
5 – Love heals me
6 – There is limitless love to give and receive
7 – All is well, I am loved

(B3) Valuable, lovable and connected
1 – I am here now
2 – I am connected to all that is, no matter what I do or feel
3 – I am valuable no matter what I do or feel
4 – I am lovable no matter what I do or feel
5 – I am completely accepted
6 – I feel this in my heart and body
7 – Thank you for everything

(B4) Noticing love
  1 – I am here now
  2 – I am completely connected to all that is
  3 – The voice in my head is silent
  4 – As I breathe love enters me
  5 – I easily sense love around me and through me
  6 – I am full of love
  7 – Thank you for everything

(B5) Seven directions
  (pick 1 or 2 aspects of each direction to focus on)
  1 – Visualize east—sunrise, wind, flying eagle, good vision and direction
  2 – visualize south—noontime, fire, grizzly bear, strength, healing
  3 – visualize west—sunset, water, deer, heart center, energy flow
  4 – visualize north—midnight, dark or full moon, earth, horse, action, change
  5 – visualize above—sky and stars or all of the universe, unconditional love
  6 – visualize below—mother earth that you stand on, wisdom, power, support
  7 – visualize inward—your spiritual presence, being fully in your body, heart, mind

(B6) I belong
1 – I am here now
2 – I am completely connected to all that is
3 – I have an unalterable right to presume on that connection
4 – I belong here, now
5 – I belong in this _____
   Examples: family, partnership, place, culture, group etc.)
   Pick one or more or use your own words
6 – I am accepted
7 – All is well, I am loved

(B7) I am alive
1 – I am here now
2 – I am completely connected to all that is
3 – I completely alive
4 – My heart, mind, body and intuition are alive
5 – As I breathe I feel alive
6 – My _____ is completely alive
   Examples: creativity, power, loving, heart, compassion, sexuality, thinking, etc. Pick one or more or another aspect of your aliveness
7 – All is well, I am loved

(B8) Whole and complete
1 – I am here, now, in my body
2 – I am connected to all life
3 – The content of that connection is unconditional love
4 – I am whole and complete no matter what I may think or feel
5 – My presence needs no justification
6 – I am whole and complete, not broken
7 – All is well, I am loved

(B9) I am a work of art
1 – I am here now
2 – I am completely connected to all that is
3 – My body is an exquisite work of art
4 – My life journey is an exquisite work of art
5 – I accept that my varied experiences will help create the art that is me
6 – I am completely involved in the creation
7 – Thank you for everything

(B10) I am valuable or worthy
1 – I am here now
2 – I am completely connected to all that is
3 – I am valuable (worthy) no matter what I have or have not done
4 – My mind is valuable
5 – My heart is valuable
6 – My body is valuable
7 – Thank you for everything

(B11) Being interrupted or ignored
1 – I am here now
2 – I am completely connected to all that is
3 – Even when I am interrupted (ignored), I am important and valuable
4 – My opinion is valuable (important)
5 – My thinking is valuable (important)
6 – My emotions are valuable (important)
7 – Thank you for everything

(B12) I am loved
1 – I am here now
2 – I am completely connected to all that is
3 – I am loved
4 – All aspects of me are valuable and worthy
5 – No matter what I think or how I feel, I am completely loved
6 – Without doubt, I am loved
7 – Thank you for everything

(B13) My love is good
1 – I am here now
2 – I am completely connected to all that is
3 – My love is good
4 – My loving is valuable and important to myself and others
5 – I don't need to achieve or to prove anything
6 – Without doubt my love is good
7 – Thank you for everything

(B14) I am not dead
1 – I am here now
2 – I am completely connected to all that is
3 – I am not dead
4 – I feel my body here now
5 – I feel my thoughts and emotions here now
6 – I am alive. I am not dead
7 – Thank you for everything

(B15) Aligning with my true nature
1 – I am here now
2 – I am completely connected to all that is
3 – My true way of being is now clear to see
4 – What my true self wants is clear to see
5 – Anything that doesn't truly match me disappears
6 – I now know what to do
7 – Thank you for everything

(B16) I am at cause
1 – I am here now
2 – I am completely connected to all that is
3 – I choose to be at cause for everything in my life
4 – I am not to blame
5 – Since I am at cause, I can change
6 – I can have the life I want
7 – Thank you for everything

(B17) I am trustworthy
1 – I am here now
2 – I am completely connected to all that is
3 – I am trustworthy
4 – I am fully honest with myself
5 – I think and act with integrity
6 – I am trustworthy
7 – Thank you for everything

C. INQUIRY – NOTICING WHAT IS REALLY TRUE FOR ME

In the inquiry exercises are repeated references to the presence of your All Knowing All Seeing self. This is your vision of a person that looks just like you and is a beneficial ally that really knows you no matter what. He or she knows everything that ever has or will happen to you and will tell you the truth when you ask. You can also substitute the image of your higher power or an animal spirit, an angel or god/goddess figure if you like.

(C1) Welcoming the All Knowing All Seeing self
    1 – I am here now
    2 – I am completely connected to all that is
    3 – I close my eyes and sense a trusted ally here
    4 – It is my All Knowing All Seeing self
    5 – (S)He knows everything about me
    6 – I easily see and hear his (her) perspective
    7 – Thank you for everything

(C2) Identifying a fear
    1 – I am here now
    2 – I am completely connected to all that is
    3 – I open myself to be seen
    4 – I sense my All Knowing All Seeing self
    5 – (S)He knows what I fear
    6 – (S)He tells me and I hear it
    7 – Thank you for everything

(C3) Noticing my magic
1 – I am here now
2 – I am completely connected to all that is
3 – I am completely connected to my love here and now
4 – I easily recognize my best gifts and abilities
5 – I embrace these as my unique magic
6 – This is where I belong
7 – Thank you for everything

(C4) Noticing signs in my environment
1 – I am here now
2 – I am completely connected to all that is
3 – As I breathe I release thought and emotion
4 – I notice all aspects of my environment here and now
5 – My environment speaks to me in my terms
6 – It is easy to interpret
7 – Thank you for everything

(C5) Paying attention
1 – I am here now
2 – I am completely connected to all that is
3 – I am slowing down to notice more
4 – Life is immense
5 – I see more, from a wider perspective
6 – I allow this new vision
7 – Thank you for everything

(C6) Listening to the All Knowing All Seeing self
1 – I am here now
2 – I am completely connected to all that is
3 – I feel the presence of my All Knowing All Seeing self (close your eyes and create a vision or picture in your mind)
4 – I trust his (her) vision to give me the most beneficial opinion
5 – I hear what (s)he has to say
6 – This is easy
7 – Thank you for everything

(C7) Listening to divine guidance
1 – I am here now
2 – I am completely connected to all that is
3 – I release all thought and emotion
4 – I feel divine presence all around me (create a vision of what it looks like)
5 – It speaks what is highest and best for me
6 – I am listening
7 – Thank you for everything

(C8) Listening to the body
1 – I am here now
2 – I am completely connected to all that is
3 – I am relaxed, open and present without reacting to fear
4 – My body is telling me what it needs
5 – I am listening
6 – I am hearing what my body truly needs
7 – All is well, I am loved

(C9) Identifying the change I truly want
1 – I am here now
2 – I am completely connected to all that is
3 – I now step into my true All Knowing Self (conscious and unconscious)
4 – All things I feel I *should* do are low priority at this time
5 – What I truly want comes easily into my mind to be noticed
6 – There it is
7 – Thank you for everything

(C10) Questioning my thoughts or beliefs
1 – I am here now
2 – I am completely connected to all that is
3 – I am looking at my belief about _____
4 – I welcome my All Knowing All Seeing self as an ally
5 – Together we can easily see if _____ matches my true values or perspective
6 – I have my answer
7 – Thank you for everything

(C11) Is this really mine?
1 – I am here now
2 – I am completely connected to all that is
3 – I am looking at my belief about _____
4 – I welcome my All Knowing All Seeing self as an ally
5 – We can easily see if this belief (feeling, behavior – *pick one*) belongs to me
6 – I now know
7 – Thank you for everything

(C12) True, not true or maybe true?

1 – I am here now
2 – I am completely connected to all that is
3 – I am here with my All Knowing All Seeing self
4 – I have a question and my thinking mind is on a break
5 – I ask my All Knowing All Seeing self: is _____ (state the question) true, not true, or maybe true for me?
6 – I trust and accept the answer
7 – Thank you for everything

(C13) How am I at cause?

1 – I am here now
2 – I am completely connected to all that is
3 – I am here with my All Knowing All Seeing self
4 – Without shame I accept that I create all of my life
5 – (S)He tells me how I am at cause
6 – There is always something to learn or accept
7 – Thank you for everything

You can follow with Exercise **B15–Aligning with my true nature**

(C14) Checking for permission

1 – I am here now
2 – I am completely connected to all that is
3 – I sense my All Knowing All Seeing self (notice what this feels like)
4 – (S)He knows what is true
5 – I ask "do I have permission from all of myself for _____"
6 – However this feels, I trust the answer
7 – Thank you for everything

C. Inquiry – Noticing What Is Really True For Me 97

(C15) My body (heart or spirit) has the answer
 1 – I am here now
 2 – I am completely connected to all that is
 3 – My body (heart or spirit) will tell me what is true
 4 – Just for now my thinking mind is on a break
 5 – I listen as my body (heart or spirit) speaks
 6 – I notice what my body (heart or spirit) says to me
 7 – Thank you for everything

(C16) Identifying my true beliefs
 1 – I am here now
 2 – I am completely connected to all that is
 3 – I am here with my All Knowing All Seeing self
 4 – Together we easily see what matches my true nature and values
 5 – I now see my true point of view
 6 – I have full permission to hold on to this view
 7 – Thank you for everything

(C17) Identifying my true needs
 1 – I am here now
 2 – I am fully connected to all that is
 3 – I now step into my true all knowing self conscious and unconscious)
 4 – I easily see what I truly need about _____
   Examples: time, attention, touch, sex, education, community, connection, food, sleep, fun, relaxation, information etc. Pick one or use your own
 5 – I easily see my *true* needs
 6 – I have full permission to know and keep this perspective (it may help to write this down)
 7 – Thank you for everything

(C18) Identifying my true needs instead of sex
    1 – I am here now
    2 – I am fully connected to all that is
    3 – I allow myself to feel that I need sex now
        (one breath only)
    4 – I envision this feeling as a distinct form outside of my body
    5 – I put that feeling aside (envision a safe friend holding it for you)
    6 – I now see and accept what I truly need
        (attention, nurturing, touch, rest, etc)
    7 – Thank you for everything

(C19) Noticing how I eat
    1 – I am here now
    2 – I am completely connected to all that is
    3 – As I eat, I notice if I am all here
    4 – I notice what I am eating
    5 – I notice how fast and how much I eat
    6 – I notice how eating affects me
    7 – Thank you for everything

(C20) Finding what I want
    1 – I am here now
    2 – I am completely connected to all that is
    3 – I now step into my true All Knowing Self
        (conscious and unconscious)
    4 – I have full permission to see what I want
    5 – The vision is forming
    6 – I want _____
    7 – Thank you for everything

(C21) What works best
   1 – I am here now
   2 – I am completely connected to all that is
   3 – I am clear and present in my mind and body
      (If you cannot get clear go to a clearing exercise)
   4 – My All Knowing All Seeing self is here as my ally
   5 – I easily see what serves me and my situation best
   6 – I get to choose
   7 – Thank you for everything

(C22) Identifying my authentic desires
   1 – I am here now
   2 – I am completely connected to all that is
   3 – I now step into my true All Knowing Self
      (conscious and unconscious)
   4 – I easily see my true desires distinct from any that belong to others
   5 – There they are
   6 – I have full permission to know and keep this perspective
   7 – Thank you for everything

(C23) Finding all of my story
   1 – I am here now
   2 – I am completely connected to all that is
   3 – I now step into my true All Knowing Self
      (conscious and unconscious)
   4 – I want _____ to change
   5 – Just for now, the voice in my head is silent
   6 – Any story that hinders what I want rises to be recognized
   7 – Thank you for everything

(C24) Checking for unknown blocks

1 – I am here now
2 – I am completely connected to all that is
3 – I now step into my true All Knowing Self (conscious and unconscious)
4 – I want _____ to change
5 – Just for now, the voice in my head is silent and I don't need to understand
6 – Any block or automatic stop that I have rises to be recognized
7 – Thank you for everything

(C25) What doesn't align?

1 – I am here now
2 – I am completely connected to all that is
3 – My All Knowing All Seeing self shows me what is true
4 – I am committed to full internal alignment
5 – Thoughts or feelings that do not match me show up to be seen
6 – They are easy to identify
7 – Thank you for everything

(C26) Is this really mine?

1 – I am here now
2 – I am completely connected to all that is
3 – I am looking at my belief about _____
4 – I welcome my All Know All Seeing self
5 – We easily see if this belief (feeling, behavior, *pick one*) belongs to me
6 – I now know
7 – Thank you for everything

D. MOVING THROUGH

(D1) Bane of fear
1 – I am here now
2 – I am completely connected to all that is
3 – I now recognize my fear based thinking
4 – I see that it affects my beliefs and behavior
5 – Just for now I welcome the fear in all it's intensity knowing it will pass quickly
6 – I now allow myself to release the fear from my mind, heart and body
7 – I am still here, all is well

(D2) Moving through a feeling
1 – I am here now
2 – I am completely connected to all that is
3 – I welcome _____
   Examples: fear, pain, grief, jealousy, anger, frustration, sadness, loss, missing, hopelessness, helplessness, powerlessness, overwhelm, surprise, etc.
4 – I fully allow myself to feel it for as long as it takes
5 – I allow the feeling to pass through me
6 – I notice the change as it goes away
7 – Thank you for everything

(D3) Moving through resistance
 1 – I am here now
 2 – I am completely connected to all that is
 3 – I feel resistance to this change
 4 – I feel to the immense flow of life and allow movement
 5 – I hold no limitations
 6 – I feel the shift inside
 7 – Thank you for everything

(D4) Moving through stuckness
 1 – I am here now
 2 – I am completely connected to all that is
 3 – I see myself, and where I am frozen or stuck (close your eyes and envision your body with stuck/frozen place(s)
 4 – I envision supportive beings all around me
 5 – They breathe into my frozen place(s) to create movement
 6 – Slowly, gently, as my body begins to thaw, I see what I can do or allow to be different (take your time with this one)
 7 – Thank you for everything

(D5) Moving through a fear or difficulty
 1 – I am here now
 2 – I am completely connected to all that is
 3 – I breathe in my fear or difficulty about _____
 4 – I welcome any feeling (even if it is uncomfortable)
 5 – I have all the time I need (stay with the feeling)
 6 – I watch as the feelings pass and my point of view changes
 7 – Thank you or everything

(D6) Moving through dis-ease
1 – I am here now
2 – I am completely connected to all that is
3 – I welcome a clear vision of my disease now
4 – I make a sound (humming) and see my body release the dissonance
5 – My body is fully able to heal
6 – I am filled with radiant energy
7 – Thank you for everything

(D7) Moving through emotion
1 – I am here now
2 – I am completely connected to all that is
3 – I am completely safe
4 – I welcome my _____ (say your emotion)
   Examples: fear, anger, hate, lust, joy, ecstasy, overwhelm, worry etc.
5 – I allow my emotion to be here for as long as it is helpful
6 – I now allow my emotion to move and change
7 – Thank you for everything

E. RELEASE

(E1) Releasing fear
   1 – I am here now
   2 – I am completely connected to all that is
   3 – I recognize my fear
   4 – I notice where my fear rests in my body
   5 – I breathe out all the fear from my body, heart and mind
   6 – Fire (water, wind, earth – *pick one*) takes it from me
   7 – All is well, I am loved

(E2) Release with body movement while standing
   1 – I am here now
   2 – I am completely connected to all that is
   3 – Inhale: Your open hands aim at the ground and move up past the body to full upward extension as you inhale slowly. Picture cleansing, alive energy flowing up through you from mother earth.
   4 – Exhale: Your open hands travel past your head and the rest of your body to aim at the earth as you exhale slowly: See the tension release from any part of you and flow to mother earth for recycling into love.
   5 – Repeat 3
   6 – Repeat 4
   7 – Thank you for everything

(E3) Releasing carried perspective (without a story)
1 – I am here now
2 – I am completely connected to all that is
3 – I release any perspective I carry that I don't need
4 – I don't need to understand
5 – I feel it leave my mind and body
6 – This is permanent
7 – Thank you for everything

(E4) Releasing stuckness
1 – I am here now
2 – I am completely connected to all that is
3 – I locate the feel of stuckness in my body
4 – I am bathed in the relaxing, forgiving breath of spirit
5 – Stuckness dissipates
6 – I welcome new vision
7 – Thank you for everything

(E5) Releasing all blockage to change
1 – I am here now
2 – I am completely connected to all that is
3 – I am in charge – I have full permission
4 – I want _____ (say the change you want)
5 – Whether or not I understand, I release all blocks to this change
6 – I release them permanently
7 – Thank you for everything

(E6) Release of a heart connection (close your eyes)
   1 – I am here now
   2 – I choose to release my heart connection to _____ (say the name)
   3 – I feel the powerful presence of sacred bear energy (or a trusted ally) holding me
   4 – I see _____ (say the name of person) moving away on the back of a horse.
   5 – With a knife, the bear (or trusted ally) cuts the connection between us
   6 – I am still here and I feel the difference
   7 – Thank you for everything

(E7) Releasing
   1 – I am here now
   2 – I am completely connected to all that is
   3 – I completely release _____
      (As you say this, visualize. What does release look like? For example, it flies away – it explodes – it dissipates in air or water – it burns up – it is buried – someone you trust takes it – it stops having power, it deflates)
   4 – That was easy
   5 – I no longer carry _____
   6 – I feel different without it (notice how)
   7 – Thank you for everything

(E8) Releasing emotion
1 – I am here now
2 – I am completely connected to all that is
3 – I release the feeling of _____
4 – I watch and breathe as _____ drains out of my body
5 – I feel different as it leaves
6 – I am returning to my normal balance
7 – Thank you for everything

(E9) Release of emotion 2
1 – I am here now
2 – I am completely connected to all that is
3 – I recognize my feelings of _____
   Examples: fear, hopelessness, jealousy, competition, anger, overwhelm, hurt, sadness, etc.
4 – My _____ no longer serves me well
5 – I release _____ from my body, heart and mind
6 – I feel the shift
7 – Thank you for everything

(E10) Release of control
1 – I am here now
2 – I am completely connected to all that is
3 – I do not need to control the situation
4 – I release control
5 – However I feel, all is proceeding as it should
6 – I completely release control
7 – Thank you for everything

(E11) Release of control 2
1 – I am here now
2 – I am completely connected to all that is
3 – All is unfolding as it should
4 – I have no need to control the situation or the people involved
5 – However I feel, my life is working well
6 – I release all control
7 – All is well, I am loved

(E12) Release of a secret
1 – I am here now
2 – I am completely connected to everything (close your eyes)
3 – I feel where this secret resides in my body
4 – I feel the strong loving spirit of a bear (or trusted ally) here
5 – With both hands I remove this secret and give it to bear (or ally)
6 – It is gone, I am no longer burdened
7 – Thank you for everything

(E13) Release of shame or guilt
1 – I am here now
2 – I am completely connected to all that is
3 – I feel my shame (guilt) in my body
4 – As I look, it turns into a ball of energy
5 – With both hands, I remove it from my body and place it on the ground
6 – I step away and watch it explode into ashes and blow away
7 – Thank you for everything

F. WELCOMING GOALS AND CHANGES – ACTIVITIES

(F1) Having it all
1 – I am here now
2 – I am completely connected to all that is
3 – The substance of that connection is unconditional love
4 – There are no limits to what is possible
5 – This means _____ (you may want to write this down)
6 – From this moment foreword, I choose to keep this belief (vision, choice)
7 – Thank you for everything

(F2) Filling with energy with body movement while standing
1 – I am here now
2 – Inhale: your open hands aim at the ground and move up to your chest, palms facing each other, one foot apart as you inhale slowly. Picture alive active energy flowing into you from mother earth
3 – Exhale: picture a ball of radiant golden energy between your hands as you exhale slowly
4 – Inhale: Move hands to your chest. Bring the image of that energy ball into your chest
5 – Exhale: Feel it inside you
6 – Repeat 2-5 times until your feel full of energy
7 – Thank you for everything

(F3) Filling with energy with body movement while standing 2

1 – Inhale: your open hands aim at the ground and move up to your chest, palms facing yourself, 6-12 inches away as you inhale slowly. Picture alive active energy coming up from mother earth.
2 – Exhale: picture yourself filling up like a glass of water
3 – Repeat 1 and 2 until you are full

(F4) I am at cause 2

1 – I am here now
2 – I am completely connected to all that is
3 – I chose to be at cause for everything in my life
4 – I am not to blame
5 – Since I am at cause, I can change anything
6 – This means _____ (create a new vision or steps toward change now)
7 – Thank you for everything

(F5) I am awake – I have energy

1 – I am here now
2 – I am completely connected to all that is
3 – As I breathe a little deeper, I invite energy into my body
4 – I accept energy from my surroundings into my body (hand motion directs energy up into your body from the earth)
5 – I am awake and balanced
6 – I automatically continue to breathe a little deeper
7 – Thank you for everything

(F6) Slowing down
1 – I am here now
2 – I am completely connected to all that is
3 – As I breathe I am slowing down
4 – The little voice in my head is on a break
5 – My body is resting
6 – I am happy to be going slowly
7 – Thank you for everything

(F7) Welcoming my intuition
1 – I am here now
2 – I am completely connected to all that is
3 – I release any thought or emotion
4 – I open to notice and receive intuitive input
5 – It is easy to identify
6 – I accept this way of communication
7 – Thank you for everything

(F8) Claiming health (finding health, or being healthy)
1 – I am here now
2 – I am completely connected to all that is
3 – I have all I need to be completely healthy
4 – All changes I need in diet, lifestyle, thinking or relationships are becoming clear and apparent to me
5 – I release all fear-based thoughts
6 – I welcome these changes
7 – All is well, I am loved

(F9) Healing the body
    1 – I am here now
    2 – I am completely connected to all that is
    3 – My body is healing
    4 – Loving energy embraces the hurt place
    5 – Loving attention allows me to heal quickly
    6 – Rapid healing continues as I rest and focus on other things
    7 – Thank you for everything

(F10) Healing the body 2
    1 – I am here now
    2 – I am completely connected to all that is
    3 – My body is healing
    4 – _____ (name your ailment) is disappearing
    5 – Strength returns
    6 – Balance returns
    7 – Thank you for everything

(F11) Healing the heart
    1 – I am here now
    2 – I am completely connected to all that is
    3 – My heart is healing
    4 – It's OK not to figure it out
    5 – I am held in love (picture loving ally(s) – people or animal spirits)
    6 – I steadily come back to balance
    7 – Thank you for everything

(F12) Healing another
1 – I am here now
2 – I am completely connected to all that is
3 – _____ (who or what) is healing
4 – _____ (name the ailment) is disappearing
5 – Strength returns
6 – Balance returns
7 – Thank you for everything

(F13) Relaxed and sleepy
1 – I am here now
2 – I am completely connected to all that is
3 – As I breathe I release all thought
4 – As I breathe my body releases all tension
5 – I am becoming relaxed and sleepy
6 – I peacefully surrender to rest.
7 – I am sleeping (not necessary to be conscious for this one!)

(F14) Welcoming (also see Chapter 4 to design your own)
1 – I am here now
2 – I am completely connected to all that is
3 – I now welcome _____ (say what you want)
4 – I breathe _____ into my heart and body and mind
5 – This is easy
6 – Life offers me just what I need
7 – Thank you for everything

(F15) Welcoming a feeling
1 – I am here now
2 – I am completely connected to all that is
3 – I welcome the feeling of _____
4 – I allow it into my body and heart and mind
5 – It is mine
6 – I welcome _____
7 – Thank you for everything

(F16) Hearing life's call
1 – I am here now
2 – I am completely connected to all that is
3 – There is something to do or be that matches me perfectly
4 – I hear it and know it
5 – It fills me and satisfies me
6 – I feel the truth in it
7 – Thank you for everything

(F17) Responding to life's call
1 – I am here now
2 – I am completely connected to all that is
3 – I choose to respond to _____ (what you are being called to do)
4 – I gently allow this new direction into myself
5 – I now notice 1 thing to do differently to invite this change
6 – I choose to welcome this new behavior
7 – Thank you for everything

(F18) Choosing a new habit (changing a habit)
1 – I am here now
2 – I am completely connected to all that is
3 – I _____ (state new habit as a present time truth)
   Example: I eat slowly
4 – I easily accept this new habit
5 – I _____ (say new habit again)
6 – This change is easy
7 – Thank you for everything

(F19) Inviting change
1 – I am here now
2 – I am completely connected to all that is
3 – I want _____ (say what you want that is new)
4 – I visualize my life with _____ already happening
5 – I easily breathe this into my mind and heart and body
6 – I trust life to make my path obvious
7 – Thank you for everything

(F20) Passionate living
1 – I am here now
2 – I am completely connected to all that is
3 – I am passionate!
4 – I know my passions (list 1 or more)
5 – I invite (10 minutes up to hours) of passionate activity each day
6 – This commitment feeds my heart
7 – Thank you for everything

(F21) Stepping into change now
1 – I am here now
2 – I am completely connected to all that is
3 – I am changing my life to include _____ (say what you want that is new)
4 – This means _____
(with at least 4 breaths, allow yourself to find the easiest and best way to step into this change and write it down)
5 – I commit to _____ (choose small steps you can realistically achieve)
6 – I continue to see the best pathway
7 – Thank you for everything

(F22) Contradicting old beliefs
1 – I am here now
2 – I am completely connected to all that is
3 – I used to believe _____ (state your old belief)
4 – Now I choose to believe _____ (state your new choice simply)
5 – This means _____ (how you will benefit)
6 – This also means _____ (one thing you will do differently)
7 – Thank you for everything

G. WELCOMING NEW PERSPECTIVE – STATE OF BEING

(G1) All is proceeding as it should
1 – I am here
2 – I am connected to all life
3 – I am safe
4 – Even if I am _____ (afraid, stressed, angry, hurt etc.) I know that all is proceeding as it should
5 – I am at peace
6 – Thank you for everything
7 – All is well, I am loved

(G2) Welcoming what is happening
1 – I am here now
2 – I am completely connected to all that is
3 – I see what is really happening
4 – I don't need to understand
5 – I don't need to agree
6 – I am safe and see what is happening
7 – Thank you for everything

(G3) Welcoming new perspective
1 – I am here now
2 – I am completely connected to all that is
3 – I breathe in this new point of view
4 – Even if it feels unusual, I accept it
5 – This is easy
6 – I allow this change
7 – Thank you for everything

(G4) Coming from the "I love you" place
 1 – I am here now
 2 – I am completely connected to all that is
 3 – I am completely safe
 4 – I realize the unconditional love I hold for all beings
 5 – Even with unresolved emotions, I still have love
 6 – I remain loving
 7 – Thank you for everything

(G5) Welcoming a person or situation
 1 – I am here now
 2 – I am completely connected to all that is
 3 – I can stay safe and welcome this person (situation)
 4 – I am only influenced when I choose to be
 5 – I am at cause
 6 – I will remain safe
 7 – Thank you for everything

(G6) Balanced while loving
 1 – I am here now
 2 – I am completely connected to all that is
 3 – I am loving fully and keeping my choice
 4 – I see the other's perspective as separate and valuable
 5 – I am still caring well for me
 6 – I am safe and balanced
 7 – Thank you for everything

(G7) Allowing what I want
1 – I am here now
2 – I am completely connected to all that is
3 – I have complete permission to have what I want
4 – This will not harm me or anyone else
5 – I lovingly allow my desire to become a vision
6 – I welcome this vision into my heart
7 – Thank you for everything

(G8) Creating a vision
1 – I am here now
2 – I am completely connected to all that is
3 – I am alive with my new desire
4 – I now envision what I want with great detail (it may help to write this down)
5 – I allow this vision to flow into my heart, mind, and body
6 – I am keeping this vision
7 – Thank you for everything

(G9) Allowing vision without limits
1 – I am here now
2 – I am completely connected to all that is
3 – Just for now I am looking beyond practical limits
4 – Anything is possible
5 – I am seeing a new vision of everything I desire
6 – I am keeping this vision
7 – Thank you for everything

(G10) Quieting the little voice
1 – I am here now
2 – I am completely connected to all that is
3 – The little voice in my head is on a break
4 – This is a relief (easy, good – pick one)
5 – No harm will come to me
6 – I welcome this break. It will last for _____ (mins. hrs. days)
7 – Thank you for everything

(G11) Welcoming emotion
1 – I am here now
2 – I am completely connected to all that is
3 – I am completely safe
4 – I welcome my _____ (fear, anger, hate, lust, joy, ecstasy, overwhelm, worry etc.)
5 – I allow my emotion to be here for as long as it is helpful
6 – I allow my emotion to move and change
7 – Thank you for everything

(G12) Safety while feeling emotion
1 – I am here now
2 – I am completely connected to all that is
3 – Even though I feel fear, _____ (sadness, pain, anxiety, etc.), I am safe
4 – No harm will come to me
5 – This is my decision
6 – I am completely safe
7 – Thank you for everything

G. Welcoming new perspective – state of being

(G13) Keeping Safe
  1 – I am here now
  2 – I am completely connected to all that is
  3 – I carry my safety with me, it is my decision
  4 – I know what to do or not do to stay safe
  5 – I commit to keeping safe
  6 – I am safe
  7 – I am loved, Thank you for everything

(G14) This is easy
  1 – I am here now
  2 – I am completely connected to all that is
  3 – This is easy
  4 – I breathe into ease
  5 – I feel completely supported (from all directions)
  6 – This will continue to be easy
  7 – Thank you for everything

(G15) I choose this life
  1 – I am here now
  2 – I am completely connected to all that is
  3 – I choose this life
  4 – Thank you for everything
  5 – I accept that I am creating every part of my journey
  6 – I choose this life
  7 – All is well. I am loved.

(G16) Giving myself permission
   1 – I am here now
   2 – I am completely connected to all that is
   3 – I invite my unconscious mind to listen
   4 – I have permission to _____ (say what you want to do or be)
   5 – However this feels I still have permission
   6 – I notice the change
   7 – Thank you for everything

(G17) No limits
   1 – I am here now
   2 – I am completely connected to all that is
   3 – The substance of that connection is unconditional love
   4 – There are no limits to what is possible
   5 – This means _____ (you may want to write this down)
   6 – From this moment foreword I choose to keep this belief
   7 – Thank you for everything

(G18) Accepting the love all around me
   1 – I am here now
   2 – I am completely connected to all that is
   3 – Love is actually all around
   4 – There is more than enough
   5 – I breathe in love
   6 – Love enters me and affects (heals, fills, changes) me
   7 – Thank you for everything

(G19) I am treated well
1 – I am here now
2 – I am completely connected to all that is
3 – I am treated well
4 – I am OK just the way I am
5 – My ease and self acceptance is obvious to everyone
6 – I am treated well
7 – Thank you for everything

(G20) Life is easy
1 – I am here now
2 – I am completely connected to all that is
3 – Life is easy
4 – I have everything I need
5 – My heart and mind are open to receive from unexpected sources
6 – I have ease and contentment
7 – Thank you for everything

(G21) Peaceful and relaxed
1 – I am here now
2 – I am completely connected to all that is
3 – I feel my body relax
4 – I release attachment to my thoughts
5 – I feel my heart relax
6 – I am at peace
7 – Thank you for everything

(G22) Solid and grounded
  1 – I am here now
  2 – I am completely connected to all that is
  3 – I feel my feet connected to the earth
      (it helps to put your bare feet on the earth)
  4 – I am being held by my planet
  5 – I feel the solid steady vibration of the earth
  6 – I breathe in rhythm with the earth
  7 – Thank you for everything

(G23) I am honest with myself
  1 – I am all here now
  2 – I am now totally honest with myself
  3 – What is true shows up to be noticed
  4 – Anything hidden shows up to be noticed
  5 – Even if scary or overwhelming I accept myself
  6 – I am comfortable with all of me
  7 – Thank you for everything

(G24) I am honest with others even if scared
  1 – I am all here now
  2 – I am completely connected to all that is
  3 – I am completely honest with others
  4 – I value honesty more than my emotional response
  5 – I will survive and thrive
  6 – I will remain safe
  7 – Thank you for everything.

(G25) I trust myself
   1 – I am here now
   2 – I am completely connected to all that is
   3 – I am fully connected to my best, balanced thinking
   4 – I can ask for help
   5 – My emotions do not control all of my behavior
   6 – I trust myself
   7 – Thank you for everything

(G26) Open to receive
   1 – I am here now
   2 – I am completely connected to all that is
   3 – I am open to receive something new
   4 – My mind welcomes the newness
   5 – My heart is safe and open
   6 – I feel *new and different* flowing into me
   7 – Thank you for everything

(G27) Inviting magic
   1 – I am here now
   2 – I am completely connected to life and love here and now
   3 – I fully accept that all is possible
   4 – I want _____
   5 – I accept that life responds in it's own way
   6 – I am open to see and accept what life offers
   7 – Thank you for everything

(G28) Inviting oneness, full connection and ecstasy
  1 – I am here now
  2 – I am completely connected to all that is
  3 – I am completely connected to love here and now
  4 – This moment I am fully joined with _____
    (person, place, emotion, state of being, etc.)
  5 – I can feel that connection – heart, body, mind
  6 – This is ecstasy
  7 – Thank you for everything

(G29) Enough Time
  1 – I am here now
  2 – I am completely connected to all that is
  3 – I have all the time I need
  4 – I have time to think, feel, decide and do
  5 – I have time to _____
    Examples: reclaim my health, be with my kids, take care of details, get some loving attention, relax, etc. Pick one or use your own words. Repeat breath 5 once for each item
  6 – I have all the time I need
  7 – All is well; I am loved

(G30) Altering time
  1 – I am here now
  2 – I am completely connected to all that is
  3 – I have all the time I need
  4 – I invite time to change to accommodate my needs
  5 – As I alter my view of time, time alters for me
  6 – It is done
  7 – All is well; thank you for everything

G. Welcoming new perspective – state of being

(G31) Aligning the conscious and subconscious
1 – I am here now
2 – I am completely connected to all that is
3 – I want _____
4 – I have complete permission in all areas (mind, body and spirit)
5 – I release all resistance with or without a story
6 – I feel the change in me
7 – Thank you for everything

(G32) Linking success with my values
1 – I am here now
2 – I am completely connected to all that is
3 – I want _____
4 – Succeeding at this also supports my personal value of _____
5 – They go together well
6 – My vision of success includes both
7 – Thank you for everything

H. GRATITUDE AND FORGIVENESS

(H1) Gratitude about a difficulty
1 – I am here now
2 – I am completely connected to all that is
3 – I am grateful for _____ (list three positive attributes of your life – breathe once with each)
4 – I am grateful for _____ (list one difficult or challenging experience you are having)
Pause here to have feelings if they are coming up. Afterwards, repeat 4 if feelings have come up.
5 – I will keep the loving truth that I learn from this experience.
6 – I am grateful for (my) life
7 – I am loved, all is well

(H2) Gratitude
1 – I am here now
2 – I am completely connected to all that is
3 – I am grateful for _____ (list three positive attributes or beings in your life – breathe once with each)
4 – I am grateful for _____ (list three more)
5 – Thank you for everything
6 – I am grateful for (my) life
7 – All is well, I am loved

H. Gratitude and forgiveness 129

(H3) Thank you for everything
    1 – Thank you for everything
    2 – Thank you for everything
    3 – Thank you for everything
    4 – Thank you for everything
    5 – Thank you for everything
    6 – Thank you for everything
    7 – Thank you for everything

(H4) Thanks for healing
    1 – I am here now
    2 – I am completely connected to all that is
    3 – My _____ (name your ailment) is healing
    4 – Thank you for healing
    5 – I gratefully allow my body to heal
    6 – I allow all the help I need
    7 – Thank you for everything

(H5) Forgiving myself
    1 – I am here now
    2 – I am completely connected to all that is
    3 – I forgive myself
    4 – I release all negative self judgment
        (watch it fly away or disappear)
    5 – Even if I have made mistakes, I completely forgive myself
    6 – As I forgive myself my balance and power return
        (notice the signs that this is true)
    7 – I am loved, thank you for everything

(H6) Forgiving myself 2
1 – I am here now
2 – I am completely connected to all that is
3 – I see the place in my body that I hold blame of myself
4 – I envision the shape, color and size of what I hold without an explanation
5 – With both hands, I gently remove it and give it to mother earth
6 – I am completely forgiven
7 – Thank you for everything

(H7) Forgiving myself 3
1 – I am here now
2 – I am completely connected to all that is
3 – _____ is what I judge myself most harshly about
4 – I feel the burden of the weight of that judgment
5 – The spirit of the bear removes the weight from me
6 – I am completely forgiven.
7 – Thank you for everything

(H8) Forgiving others
1 – I am here now
2 – I am completely connected to all that is
3 – I forgive you
4 – I release all negative thought or judgment (visualize as it flies away or disappears)
5 – I completely forgive you
6 – As I forgive you, my balance and power return (notice the signs that this is true)
7 – I am loved, thank you for everything

(H9) Forgiveness
   1 – I am here now
   2 – I am completely connected to all that is
   3 – I love you
   4 – I forgive you
   5 – Please forgive me
   6 – Thank you for everything

More books from River Sanctuary Publishing...

The Emerald Tablets for 2012 & Beyond...ancient wisdom rewritten for the present-time truth seeker, by Ashalyn and Thoth the Atlantean, 2011. $19.95

Affirmations for Everyday Living: Create more clarity, success, and joy in your life, by Annie Elizabeth, 2010. $17.95

The Unorthodox Life: Walking Your Own Path to the Divine, by Kathy McCall, 2009. $15.95

Notes to Self: Meditations on Being, by Christy Deena, 2011. $15.95

A Space Between: Adventures and Lessons Between Lives, by Ardeth DeVries, 2010. $13.95

How Alternation Can Change Your Life: Finding the Rhythms of Health and Happiness, by Andrew Oser, 2010. $15.95

Available from:
www.riversanctuarypublishing.com

River Sanctuary Publishing
P.O. Box 1561
Felton, California 95018
www.riversanctuarypublishing.com

We offer custom book design and production with worldwide availability through print-on-demand, with the best author-friendly terms in the industry. Specializing in inspirational, spiritual and self-help books, biography, and memoirs.

www.ingramcontent.com/pod-product-compliance
Lightning Source LLC
LaVergne TN
LVHW051129080426
835510LV00018B/2312